Marvelously
MADE

Gratefulness and the Body

Marvelously
MADE

Gratefulness and the Body

Mary C. Earle

Morehouse Publishing
NEW YORK · HARRISBURG · DENVER

Quotations from the Psalter are taken from The Book of Common Prayer. All other Scripture quotations are from The New Revised Standard Version Bible, copyright © 1989 by the Division of Christian Education of the National Council of Churches of Christ in the U.S.A. Used by permission. All rights reserved.

Morehouse Publishing, 4775 Linglestown Road, Harrisburg, PA 17112

Morehouse Publishing, 445 Fifth Avenue, New York, NY 10016

Morehouse Publishing is an imprint of Church Publishing Incorporated.

www.churchpublishing.org

Cover design by Laurie Klein Westhafer
Typeset by Rose Design

A catalog record for this title is available from the Library of Congress.

ISBN: 978-0-8192-2762-1 (pbk.)
ISBN: 978-0-8192-2763-8 (ebook)

Printed in the United States of America

10 9 8 7 6 5 4 3 2 1

For my sister and dear friend, Susie Cohen, R.N.
For Sean Michael Hughston, 1983–2011

Accept, O Lord our thanks and praise for all that you have done for us. We thank you for the splendor of the whole creation, for the beauty of this world, for the wonder of life, and for the mystery of love.

—from *A General Thanksgiving*,
The Book of Common Prayer

Contents

PART 3

SHOWING FORTH GRATEFULNESS

Foreword by Margaret Benefiel

Once in a while, a book opens an entirely new world. *Marvelously Made: Gratefulness and the Body*, quite unexpectedly, did that for me.

For centuries Christian theologians have recognized the Book of Nature and the Book of Scripture as the two "books" of God's revelation. Humans come to know God (and themselves), this view goes, through meditating on the natural world and through reflecting on Scripture. Mary Earle awakened me to a third "book," the "Book of the Body." While technically a chapter in the Book of Nature, the human body has been routinely ignored by Christians seeking God's revelation in creation and thus, in its late rediscovery, deserves its own billing as a third book. *Marvelously Made* unveils the power of the body to reveal God.

This piercingly beautiful book starts with Earle's own journey to the discovery of the sacredness of the body. The second section invites the reader into meditations on different organs of the body. Deceptively simple, the meditations took me very deep very quickly, stripping off layer after layer of what gets between me and God. For example, the breath prayer in Chapter 4 on the lungs, "Breathe" (inhale) "in me" (exhale), cut through my defences, inviting me to freedom. As I invited God to breathe in me, I became aware of the barriers I erect, the ways in which I assume I must clean up my act before I can let God in. "How can you ask God to breathe in you when you are eating food that isn't good for you, when you are overeating, when you aren't exercising enough?" a voice within me protested. "That is precisely when you need to invite me to breathe in you," the quiet inner promptings responded. "I meet you where you are and I bring healing and freedom." As I continued to pray the breath prayer over subsequent days, I became aware of how I take my body for granted, and of how I ignore it so that I won't have to face its vulnerability: my aging, my fear of illness, my fear of dying. The meditations helped me embrace my vulnerability. In so doing, they paradoxically also helped me live with more freedom and gratitude for my body.

Mary Earle is eminently qualified to guide us on this journey. Her deep wisdom about God's manifestation in the body comes from her personal experience of living with a chronic ailment, from her theological training, and from her experience as a spiritual director and retreat leader. She knows intimately the journey of vulnerability, of befriending her body and meeting God as she gazes on God's marvelous handiwork therein. She knows how to invite us gently into the same experience.

We "cannot be grateful for what we don't notice. We cannot honor what we fail to see." These simple yet profound words from the opening of Chapter 2 continue to haunt me. I was blind to the "Book of the Body." *Marvelously Made* opened my eyes to the potential for meeting God in this unexplored territory. May this wise little book bring you the freedom, gratitude, and wholeness that it is bringing me.

Margaret Benefiel
Author of *Soul at Work*
and *The Soul of a Leader*
March 2012

Acknowledgments

This book came about as a result of my facilitating quarterly Saturday morning gatherings for exploring spirituality and health at Health Texas, a medical practice in San Antonio, at the invitation of my family practice physician, Melba Beine, M.D. Dana Martinez, R.N., has been instrumental in helping me think about topics for those gatherings, and the participants have helped me become increasingly aware of the God-given gift of our bodies.

I am grateful for the community of my home parish, St. Mark's Episcopal Church in San Antonio, Texas. Their support and encouragement of this writing vocation is a gift beyond measure.

I am indebted to the staff of Church Publishing for their flexibility and steady support along the way, especially Ryan Masteller and Nancy Bryan, and to my editor Cynthia Shattuck.

Gabrielle Marcus, massage therapist, and Damian Cortez, trainer, have offered perspective and encouragement as this book was conceived and began to take shape.

I am grateful to friends who are physicians whose wisdom and skill have shaped my own reflections: Bill Smith, David Dean, Melba Beine, Steven Cohen, Keith Eyre, Joycelyn Theard, Seema Dar, Nancy Otto, and Harry Gunkel.

My sister, Susie Cohen, R.N., has graciously read the manuscript for technical accuracy; any remaining errors are my own. Susie taught me to be amazed when the body heals.

To my husband Doug I owe profound thanks for walking with me through the physical difficulties of the last year, and for yet again being a thoughtful and encouraging first reader.

All the stories in this book are true, though the names have been changed to protect the privacy of those who generously gave me permission to relate their experiences.

PART 1

"I will thank you because I am
marvelously made"

"You Knit Me Together in My Mother's Womb"

I suppose it started with my grandfather's stethoscope. My mother's father was a physician, the kind of doctor who always carried his black medical bag with him. When my sister and I were young, Pawpaw Joe would let us play with his medical bag, under his supervision. He taught us how to find the heart. He would put the ends of the stethoscope in his ears, and quietly listen to our hearts. Then it would be our turn. Susie and I would each have an opportunity to imitate Pawpaw's actions, and discover anew that distinctive "lub-dub" within our own chests, each others', and my grandfather's.

Ever since my youth, the human body has been a miracle to me. The sheer wonder of a heart that beats steadily for a lifetime. The mystery of blood carrying nutrients and oxygen throughout a stunning array of capillaries. The quiet, miraculous work of the liver, cleansing and clearing toxins from the body. Bones growing and lengthening in an adolescent child's body. Scratches on the skin healing over, as if there had never been a wound.

When I was pregnant for the first time, I became acutely aware that within our bodies, God's own Spirit is present at every moment, creating new cells, sustaining life, healing and making organs new. I was working as a counselor for the

Department of Obstetrics and Gynecology at the University of Texas Health Science Center in San Antonio. The physicians in the department, particularly the woman infertility specialist, would stop me and ask how I was feeling, and how far along the pregnancy was. Often observations along these lines would follow: "So, this week the eyes are forming." Or, "About now, that baby's lungs are getting stronger." From this I realized that I was housing a life, a life I could support with nutrition, exercise and rest. Yet in no way was I making the baby who would later be Bryan Earle. I was cooperating, but, I was not the author of this work. Those organs, eyes, fingers, toes, ears, eyelashes, and mouth were all being brought forth and shaped by Life working within this particular life.

It began to occur to me that what was so explicitly true with a pregnancy was also true with our day-to-day bodily life. Within the confines of our bodies we house organs and systems that are, at every moment, instruments for creating and sustaining life. Minute by minute, breath by breath, heartbeat by heartbeat, our earthly lives are the manifestation of wondrous physicality, a physicality that is God-given and God-embraced in Jesus. As the author of the psalms proclaimed so long ago, "You yourself created my inmost parts" (Ps. 139:12).

In exploring our bodies, our physicality, my sister Susie has helped me along the way. As a registered nurse she worked first in pediatric oncology and then with adults, now she is a labor and delivery nurse. From time to time we have yet another conversation about the body. Despite all that she has witnessed in the world of oncology, all of the rigors of cancer treatment, Susie remains astounded by the capacity of the body to work wonders at every moment. Not so long ago she called to say, "Kidneys! Can you believe what a kidney can do! How does a kidney regulate pH in the blood? How is it that those two organs know how to regulate the fluid in the body?" Susie's ability to be astonished by the body's capacity to function at all has given me guidance along the way. She receives the body as a gift, the various metabolic processes as an astounding reality not of our making, and her life work is an embodied offering of thanksgiving: "I will thank you because I am marvelously made" (Ps. 139:13).

All of these primary experiences of God's presence within the sanctuary of the body have led me to sense the sacredness of our physical life. Our bodies are one locus of God's creating, redeeming, and sanctifying life. They are places set aside for beholding and receiving the presence of God, a presence in which we abide. Just as we gather in sanctuaries to offer worship, so we may sit still in the sanctuary of the body, attend to our breath, and know that God is God. We may dwell within the present moment as we notice breath, touch, smell, sound, pleasure, ache, pain. Our bodies dwell in the here and now; they are our primary sanctuary for remembering God is with us and within us.

When I started going to a young mother's Bible study, and reading about religion and theology some thirty years ago, I found grounding within the Christian faith for this wonder. For at the heart of our Christian faith is the astounding confession that in Jesus, the life of God is revealed in and through a real human body. As a friend of mine used to say, "God loves bodies so much that God just had to have one." Later, when I was serving as a chaplain interviewing men and women who wanted to be ordained as priests and enter parish ministry, they were often asked questions along these lines: "Did Jesus ever have a belly ache?" "Did Jesus need diapers?" "Could Jesus have had a migraine?" The point of the questions (which sometimes created a certain amount of squirming and consternation) was to get these future clergy thinking about what is sometimes called the "scandal of the Incarnation"—that in Jesus God became a human baby. The scandal is that Jesus, the savior of the world, is truly human, truly in a body, lives human life from the inside out. One of the many contemplative dimensions of God taking on human flesh is this: Jesus reminds us that our bodies are ongoing creations. Our bodies, even when they don't work the way we want them to, are creative expressions of God's own eternal life, here and now. "Your eye beheld my limbs, yet unfinished in the womb; all of them were written in your book" (Ps. 139:14).

Today most people tend to regard the body as something to be whipped into shape through exercise, subdued and chastised through dieting, objectified as a sexual object, or simply ignored. Our Israelite ancestors knew better, realizing that our bodies are "marvelously made." Many of the psalms recognize that the sacred space of the human body is the very handiwork of God. These mortal bodies, which will "rest in hope" just as the heart and the soul rejoice (Ps. 16:9), are arranged in the most intricate and creative manner.

The fact that the organs actually communicate with each other at all is beyond my comprehension. The heart and the lungs work collaboratively at every moment, while a whole system of organs digests and transforms our food for energy and the creation of new cells. Skin and bone and muscle give us form, allow us to move, and give us sensors that tell us of our environment. Somehow, all of these organs and systems work together. Subtle hormonal and chemical signals alter our bodies, without our conscious intervention or direction. Ultimately, even for many physicians, the body remains mysterious—meaning that it cannot be fully explained. Although anatomists and physicians may describe the structure and processes of the body, the *fact* of the body's presence and capacities is beyond our cognitive grasp. Why is there something rather than nothing? How is it that bodies and matter exist? This is an occasion for contemplative receptivity, for awakening to astonishment, for giving thanks. Throughout our numbered days, God knits us together. Even in illness and trauma, we often are witnesses to the sacred space of the body, that locus of God's own presence.

I became more acutely aware of the body's contemplative potential when I began facilitating a group for Health Texas, a medical practice here in San Antonio. The physicians who own the practice began to discern a need for patients to reflect together on aspects of spirituality and health. Several years ago, I was invited to start offering Saturday morning sessions once a quarter. Any patient may attend without charge, and others are also welcome to attend. We gather, introduce ourselves, keep silence for a bit, and then reflect on material I have brought.

Very quickly I discovered that the participants vary in religious background. Most have some experience in the Christian faith, but not all, and some are of Jewish or Muslim background. Others have no link to any faith tradition or worshipping community. As a consequence, I discovered that our only "common language" was the language of the body. We all shared the basic "text" of hearts, lungs, stomachs, bones, and muscles. That is why we begin each session with the body itself. We start with basic information about how some aspect of the body works, and laugh at the fact that we know so little about these bodies that we have been given. We wonder at our bodies' ability to rebound from any variety of ailments. Occasionally we are astonished by our ignorance. Over time we have learned to "welcome the stranger" of our own bodies, slowly becoming acquainted with the mysteries within our cells, our muscles, our organs, our brains, and our blood. We encourage one another to be faithful in whatever spiritual practices that support the body's movement toward wellbeing.

I have learned from these participants that attending to the wonder of our bodies, and learning to regard our bodies with a loving and receptive contemplative awareness, leads also to increased awareness of the needs of others. Frequently we find ourselves reflecting on our assumptions as to what we expect from our health care system, and seek to remain aware of the lack of health care throughout the world. Several participants who have spent time in other countries bring to the group their experiences of places desperately in need of the essentials for life: food, clean water, clean air, and shelter. One man, who had worked in refugee camps throughout the world, has reminded us of the benefits of vaccinations, checkups, and annual blood work, all of which we can so easily take for granted. It is in this way that the members of this group have been steady witnesses to the needs of the bodies of other people throughout the world. Together we have learned that becoming aware that our bodies are "marvelously made" leads us to desiring that others' bodies receive what they need, and consequently I reflect often on these words from the gospel of Matthew: "Truly I tell you, just as you did it to one of the least of these who are members of my family, you did it to me" (Matt. 25:40). The abiding gratefulness of the participants in the group leads them to compassionate, merciful actions on the part of others. Attending to the wonder of their own physicality has led them to regard others as God's own handiwork as well.

Several sessions ago the participants were very mixed in terms of their backgrounds and beliefs. We were focusing on the lungs, and I taught them a simple breath prayer. We practiced quietly praying "Breathe" on the inhalation, and "in me" on the exhalation. Later one of them, Gina, sent me a note to say that she had used the prayer during a particularly distressing medical procedure, and that her doctor had remarked on her comparative calm. Several months after that, she left me another message saying that she continued to use the breath prayer and had taught it to her physician's nurses.

Gina's time with the other participants has led to a deepening awareness of the gift of her own lungs. She also has begun to recognize that she is an active participant in the life of her body and soul. Her care in learning the breath prayer, applying it in particular situations of medical distress, and then offering the prayer to others exemplifies what I hope will come from this book. I envision its being used in wellness centers, in prayer circles, and in all kinds of settings in which people begin to discover the gift of their bodies. It is a marvelous journey in the sense that we are led to marvel at the body as a gift of God's handiwork. The practices are also a kind of medicine that liberate us from narrow ways of understanding illness, injury, or the daily labor of the body in ordinary life.

My hope is that this book will also lead to intentional action for the wellbeing of others, as a way of giving thanks.

When we receive the good news of our bodies as sacred space, and begin to honor them as Gina has, we begin to see the implications for how we treat one another, other creatures, and the earth itself. If our bodies are so cherished by God, then all forms of abuse, rape, violence, and even self-neglect desecrate the body. Yet our culture has forgotten this completely. We who call ourselves Christians follow a way that remembers how much God loves the material world: "The Word of God, who is God, wills at all places and at all times to work the mystery of his embodiment." So wrote Maximus the Confessor in one of his treatises, the *Ambigua,* in the seventh century. The mystery of the embodiment of the life of God surrounds us within and without. God tells us in the scriptural narrative that matter is beloved and good—"God saw everything that he had made, and indeed, it was very good." (Gen. 1:31) Our bodies are good. Our bodies are living creations of the Holy One. Our bodies, so beautifully crafted and exquisitely designed, speak of the presence of God within our cells, our molecules, our atoms.

Deliver Me, O Lord

Recently I broke my wrist. The break required surgery, and it took a long, long time for full healing to take place. In the meantime, I received some of the so-called advice that passes for spiritual wisdom these days: "Breaking a bone means that something essential in you has broken down." "Breaking a hand means you can't *handle* something." Good Lord, deliver me! I said to myself. Such "advice" is far from helpful. It stops reflection and wonder in its tracks. It impedes prayer. And it is usually way off-base.

Joan Borysenko, a physician who writes on contemporary spirituality, calls this kind of interpretation "New Age fundamentalism."[1] It is a literal way of "reading" the text of the body, and invariably fails to allow the person receiving the advice to have sufficient space and time to reflect, to know, to wonder, and to pray contemplatively. Usually this shows up in the aftermath of illness or an accident, but this way of thinking about the body is also revealed in some of the ways that we have appropriated healing arts and medical practices from the east. For example, I was told when my gall bladder was removed that I'd better be prepared for anger to well up, because in Chinese herbal medicine the gall bladder is always associated with storing anger. In fact, having the diseased gall bladder removed ushered in a sense of relief and profound easing of body, mind, and spirit. The pain was gone, the liver was able to drain efficiently and my muscles eased as they unlearned their defensive postures to guard against pain. I did not find a storehouse of anger waiting to erupt. Occasionally I wonder about the cultural differences that go unremarked in our unending consumption of healing arts from other countries and traditions. It always reminds me of a line in a song by Emmylou Harris: "The surface can't tell you what the deep water knows."

Living on the surface, and feeding only on surface interpretations, we miss the depths of life and the depths of wonder. We miss the gifts being given to us at every moment. We live in an age that is beset by a variety of these fundamentalisms with regard to the body.[2] For example, a friend of mine who was diagnosed with a liver cancer was told by a family member that clearly he was not "living" to the full, presumably thinking that the noun "liver" had to do with "living." Several women I have worked with who are breast cancer survivors were also burdened with this very literal approach to the body; in their case, they were told that they had breast cancer because they were not "fully receiving their femininity." These unintentionally cruel interpretations of our embodied life are analogous to the kind of approach to sacred texts that adamantly insists on *one* way of understanding that text, and refuses the possibilities of intricacy and paradox.

As is often the case with constricted belief and practice, in this way of regarding the body x always equals y. It leaves no room for subtlety or nuance, much less wonder or mystery. Too often this way of interpreting a sacred text, or reality itself, fails to take the larger whole into account—a part is treated as if it were the whole, which leads to strange conclusions. For example, I was told that my first horrendous bout of acute pancreatitis was brought about by not being able to receive enough "sweetness" in my life, presumably because the pancreas regulates our blood sugar levels. In fact, my chronic pancreatic condition is due to a congenital malformation in the anatomy of the common bile duct. The interpretation I was given was so superficial, and not at all based in the physical reality of my own body. Deliver me, O Lord!

Sometimes we accept these facile and ready interpretations of the body because we are ignorant of the body's beauty and design. We often do not even know the basic "text" of our bodies, lacking any familiarity with the fundamentals of our own anatomy. This makes us more vulnerable to absurd or bizarre thinking about the body and about the various organs and systems. That is why learning some basics about our bodies has been truly helpful to the participants in the groups at Health Texas. We acquire knowledge about how our bodies work along with a keener sense of the interdependence of the organs. It helps us to move out of superficial ways of regarding our embodied life, and move toward knowing how much we do not know. There is a kind of freedom in letting go of false or superficial explanations and assumptions about the human body. This is the freedom to allow the body to tell its tale, to speak in that wordless language the Psalmist knew, the language of the deep structures of the cosmos:

> One day tells its tale to another,
>> and one night imparts knowledge to another.
> Although they have no words or language,
>> and their voices are not heard,
> Their sound has gone out into all lands,
>> and their message to the ends of the world.
>>
>> *(Ps. 19:2–4)*

As we listen and attend to the organs and systems of the body, we notice what is present all the time, but not seen or heard. This humbling process of discovering the extent of my own lack of awareness helps me to become less egocentric— instead of being a "know it all," I become a student who desires to be teachable. I move away from having all the answers, to realizing I don't even know the appropriate questions! As a spiritual director of mine said to me long ago, "Begin where you are, not where you are not." I begin with how little I know, and imagine the possibility of exploring this unknown inner landscape of the body, of listening for the tale the body tells.

When we begin to acquaint ourselves with the reality of the design of the body, wonder may grow. Praying "I will thank you because I am marvelously made" takes on a sturdy, grounded life. It is one thing to offer that line from Psalm 139 as a kind of generic thanksgiving for health; it is quite another to offer it after learning even a small bit about the workings of the heart, the liver, or the lungs. As we embrace this beginner's level of anatomy, we may offer these words of thanksgiving with a hearty sense of the divine creativity that has wrought our embodied life:

> And, we pray, give us such an awareness of your mercies, that we may show forth your praise, not only with our lips but in our lives, by giving up ourselves to your service, and by walking before you in holiness and righteousness all our days. (The Book of Common Prayer 101)

Learning a bit about the primary text of the body leads us into a thankful awareness of the mercies given in our daily life—the mercies of hearts that beat, lungs that breathe, stomachs and intestines that digest, brains that transmit countless messages throughout the body at any given moment. Allowing ourselves the space and time to become familiar with the sheer physical wonder of our embodied life roots our prayer within the here and now. We are drawn into the present, because that is where the body *is*. As we notice our breath, our heartbeat, our senses, our digestive life, we are more likely to be living and praying in the present moment. We discover that eternity is right here, right now, within those countless subatomic particles that make up our cells, the Life within our physical life, calling us into being at every second, out of love.

Remembering to Marvel

How to begin to receive the sacredness of your own body? In the meditations that follow in Part 2, we will focus on the anatomy of the body and the ways in which the various systems (respiratory, circulatory, digestive) function. My hope is that by starting to discover the sheer beauty and wonder of the body's design and structure, we will be drawn toward a contemplative attitude in our prayer. We will begin with deepening our awareness of our physical selves, becoming acquainted with some of the ways in which our organs labor and create, transform and cleanse the primary habitat of our bodies.

This book addresses the singular, astonishing reality that our bodies work at all. Over the years, as I have learned to live with a chronic ailment, my own gastroenterologist has helped me to perceive that amazing fact, despite the affliction. "The pancreas," she once said to me, "is still a mystery to us. It's a marvelous organ. And we really don't understand fully how it works." It was at a time when my own pancreas was laboring to recover from a severe inflammation, and I've never forgotten the corrective she offered. Start with the amazement that the body works at all. Start with the variety of functions of the pancreas. Start with the fact of your breathing, digesting, eliminating. Celebrate that wonder with patient and kindly attention to your own nutrition, water, rest, and exercise. Remember those whose bodies are not well fed, are beset by illness, or are bought and sold like commodities. Offer what you can for the well-being of the bodies of others.

My hope is that you will be led toward deeper gratefulness for the body that is yours, and that you will become more gently aware of the needs of others. This is not so much a book about healing, though it might be of help to someone living with illness, but about our bodies as God's own handiwork. I offer one way to begin noticing the wonder of our physical selves and to give thanks. It is also intended to lead us to growing compassion for others, as we recognize the sacredness of each body that God has brought forth, and remind ourselves that it is "God who has made us and not we ourselves."

Lastly, begin the day, thanking God for the sacred space of these bodies that are our primary habitat:

> For you yourself created my inmost parts;
>> you knit me together in my mother's womb.
> I will thank you because I am marvelously made;
>> your works are wonderful, and I know it well.

(Ps. 139:12–13)

2

Gratefulness for the Body

We cannot be grateful for what we do not notice, and we cannot honor what we fail to see. As simple as this might sound, we live in a society and culture that operates without the habit of gratefulness. We assume that we are entitled to receive food, water, shelter, and medical attention, and that we *will* receive them. On a political level, this definitely has validity; on the level of prayer, however, it places the self at the center of the universe. This sense of entitlement makes it so easy to overlook the sheer gift of life—the gift of being able to breathe, to stand, to walk, to eat, to be with others. It also has the subtle effect of making my needs more important than anyone else's. If my prayer life is governed by the assumption that I am entitled to life, to wellbeing, to good health, I miss so much and I become entangled in a web of self-centered thinking and behavior.

By contrast, gratefulness begins with that primary awakening—all of life is a gift. Gratefulness leads to the realization that I am not the center of the universe, but part of a vast, intricate whole. Some years ago I heard the poet and writer Maya Angelou speak at a conference. At the end of her keynote address, she accepted questions from the audience. A young person went to the microphone and asked her what

15

her basic stance of faith was. She replied, "I begin with knowing that no one owes me anything. All of life is a gift that I am called to receive." Starting to know this with respect to our bodies is an ongoing "little school for beginners," to use a phrase from the Rule of Saint Benedict. This way, this pattern of being a beginner, is steeped in realistic humility and real astonishment.

Some years ago a friend of mine, Felipe, had to have a vascular surgery in his leg. Felipe was a painter who created beautiful, huge canvases, and following his surgery, he said to me, "I realized that I have never thanked God for my legs. I could not do my art if I did not have these legs. How could I have taken this for granted for so many years?" Felipe was in his seventies when he had this little epiphany. He awakened to the gift of his legs, startled by his own failure to notice the essential role that his legs played in his vocation as artist. He was led to take further steps to honor his legs as gift, and even to paint this awareness as a form of prayer.

Growing in gratefulness begins with a desire to change our perceptions. We begin to give up the need always to be right and to be in charge. Not only can we not be grateful for what we are not able to see, *how* we see shapes *what* we see. If I choose to ignore my body, which is my primary habitat, I cannot begin to be grateful for it. If I regard my body with disdain, or with shame, I will fail to see its inherent beauty. If I only see what is "wrong" with my body (too fat or too thin, too young or too old), I fail to celebrate the body as God's own creation. What does it mean that in the United States, even in the midst of a recession, many billions are still spent on cosmetic surgery? Leaving aside reconstructive surgery following accidents or cancer operations, the majority is cosmetic As a culture, we are willing to spend vast amounts to transform our bodies into the air-brushed photograph on the cover of *Vogue* or *Elle,* a statistic pointing toward our deep ambivalence toward these bodies that we have been given for our earthly journey.

What would change for you if you were able to begin and end the day thanking God for the life of your body, for its steady continuing, for its ability to transform food into energy and breath into life for cells? What if, when beholding yourself in the mirror, you suspended your inner critic and instead asked for eyes to behold your physical self as God does? What if, upon healing from a cold or a stomach ache, you intentionally gave thanks for the body's ongoing ability to recover from the daily assault of viruses and bacteria? I invite you to notice your own embodied life, specifically the life of your unique body. As you begin to notice, you may be open to beholding your own body with the long loving look of the contemplative life. Perhaps you will allow yourself to suspend any attitudes of scorn, negligence or even disgust. Perhaps you will even be able to receive Jesus' counsel, "Do not judge, and you will not be judged; do not condemn, and you will not be condemned" (Luke 6:37).

Theologian Sallie McFague has remarked, "The most prevalent spiritual disease of our time is not wanting to be here, not wanting to be in a physical body."[3] As we allow ourselves to be healed of this malady, we become aware of our bodies. A process of befriending begins. Gratefulness takes hold. We begin to live here and now, and to see what is right in front of us.

As with any contemplative practice, the first step is to become acquainted, to pay attention. In this case, we are paying attention to the fact of the body. We are learning to listen and to watch this embodied reality that is with us every day, every night. It's harder to do this with our bodies, because we cannot get perspective. When we look in a mirror, we are seeing the reverse image of ourselves as we exist in the world. We can never really see our faces in the same way as others who behold us.

This peculiar aspect of our physical existence leads us to be mindful of our interdependence. We are created to be interdependent beings, whose lives are woven together with others. The fact of our being embodied reminds us that we are, from the very beginning, knit together both *within* a larger whole and *to* that larger whole. The body reminds us that we are intended for community, and that we are relational beings.

Furthermore, the various organs and systems, bones and nerves, work together in a collaborative way that speaks to us of divine design. In the first letter that St. Paul wrote to the church in Corinth, he remarks, "For just as the body is one and has many members, and all the members of the body, though many, are one body, so it is with Christ" (1 Cor. 12:12). Here Paul assumes the cooperative functioning of the "members," or parts of the human body. Writing in the first century, he knew that there was something truly phenomenal about the arrangement of the bodily organs and limbs, and he used that arrangement as a way to describe the church as Christ's body.

Most of us are only dimly aware of this arrangement of organs, limbs, senses, and systems. Because those organs and systems function interdependently, we are alive. Every day our bodies, quickened by breath and blood, house the life we have been given. Our bodies *are* the life we have been given. In that same letter to the Corinthians, Paul notes that our bodies are "temples of the Holy Spirit" (1 Cor. 6:19). His strong Jewish upbringing allowed him to see the body as the sacred space inhabited by God's own spirit, untroubled by later philosophical and theological doubts about the value of the body and of matter in general. Our bodies are temples, sacred spaces arranged and adorned by the design of the Holy One who breathes us into being. When we direct our attention to the ongoing gift of our bodily life, we begin to know that the uncreated life of God is at work within us—holding subatomic particles together via gravity, making us new. That life of God creates, sustains and renews our cells from day to day. We begin to recognize this physicality as gift worthy of resurrection, beloved of God, mysterious in its capacity for transformation.

How may we become more aware of the presence of God's own Spirit within these bodies? Let us reflect briefly on the ways our bodies change over time, and the ways in which we perceive those bodies. Our awareness of our bodies shifts from infancy through our later years. The five-month-old girl who lives next door to me is just discovering that she has fingers and toes, spending so much of her waking life exploring those appendages with her mouth. Watching her explore her own hands and feet, her parents smile and wonder that she is so beautifully formed.

Can you remember the first time that you became aware of your body? Hardly any of us can remember those discoveries of our infancy, but perhaps you have a recollection of the first time that you were aware of the touch of another. Perhaps you can return to a time when a parent or a friend remarked on your body, and that led you to notice it. Was there a moment in your childhood when you had a sense of wonder when a cut healed or a tooth came in? Can you recall your physical sensations in learning to ride a bicycle or jumping into a swimming pool?

How did you see your body as you became an adolescent? Sometimes the hormonal changes of teenage years startled and amazed us; sometimes we were taught to be ashamed of the physical transformations in puberty. When you recall growing and changing, having to rediscover your center of gravity on an almost daily basis, how do you remember your body? How do those perceptions differ now that you are an adult, and perhaps an adult who is in mid-life or in your latter years?

Now that I am in my sixties, I look back on the various phases that my body has lived through, and I am increasingly aware of the body's capacity to change, to heal, to be transformed. At the same time, I am noticing this body's slowing down in so many ways. When you look back, and reflect on the ways you have perceived your body over the years of your life, are there predominant themes that come forth? Do you have a particular tendency in your perspectives?

None of the cells you are beholding today, as you reflect on your own physicality, were with you in your first year of life. All of them have changed. An older friend of mine, recovering from hip surgery, remarked, "For an old girl, this body is pretty resilient. Who would have thought I'd be able to recover?" Her remark revealed awakening wonder and the stirring of deep gratefulness.

Sometimes we come to this grateful awareness through physical exercise. A new routine at the gym, once learned and practiced, may lead us to gratitude for the body's capacity to create muscle and to strengthen. Perhaps a yoga session or a qigong lesson leads us to a glimpse of the life that flows through us. Or, it could be that a walk around the block, for some unknown reason, awakens gratefulness for legs that move, a heart that beats, lungs that expand and contract. My husband Doug and I walk our three border collies (or they walk us!) almost daily, and from time to time I find myself very grateful that I can keep up with those dogs.

Others come to deepening gratefulness through those moments when the body suffers injury or illness. I have recently spent six months dealing with a broken wrist, a wrist so damaged that I was in danger of losing the use of my right hand. I had surgery. I dealt with pins that held ligaments and bones in place, and experienced stunning pain when the pins moved out of place and bore down on key nerves. I had to work to regain the use of the hand and to rebuild muscle in the right arm.

And as is so often the case, I began to truly notice my hand, wrist, and arm only after things went awry. An x-ray showed me the fine arrangement of the eight bones of the wrist, and also the damage of the fall. Thanks to my surgeon, who took the time to teach me a little anatomy of the hand, I learned about its nerves. I discovered that much of our brain's signals about sensory input are linked to the hands, so when the hand hurts, the pain registered by the brain is disproportionately acute.

Before I fell and the injury occurred, it was not the case that I had ignored my hands. As a gardener, I use them all the time. As a writer, I type and I hold a pen; as a knitter and a spinner, my fingers are used to handling all kinds of fiber. As a cook, my hands are necessary to the preparation of food. A couple of years ago, I read an online article in which the author pondered which body part she might miss the most; that led me to start thanking God for my hands.

Yet it was the loss of the use of the right hand for months that led me to a deeper gratefulness. As I observed my hand slowly beginning to respond to my attempts to hold a pen, open the refrigerator door, or take hold of a glass, I was also struck that, though I was trying to support the healing, I was not creating the new cells. In a mysterious way, the body itself was healing damaged nerves, restoring muscle, ligament, and bone, apart from anything I could do. Most of the time, my main responsibility seemed to be supporting what was unfolding in God's time and rhythm. The injury, surgery, and subsequent recovery brought something that until then had been in the background into sharp focus: every day, at any given moment, our bodies are making new cells. Every day, at any given moment, our bodies are transforming air and food into energy. Every day, at any given moment, often with little help from me, this body goes about this business of recreation. Scientists now tell us our cellular life is in a constant state of renewal. Cell division creates new cells, while old cells die off and are eliminated. New cells are formed at an astounding rate. We are in a perpetual state of being recreated on a sub-atomic and microscopic level. Yet we fail to attend to this.

In my own case, my hand will never be what it was before the fall. At the same time, I have almost full use of it. The surgeon's skill put things back together. Then new cells of bone, ligament, muscle and nerve began forming and, over time, the hand began to function again. It felt more and more reconnected to the arm and to the rest of the body. Signals from the brain began to result in a response. As I behold my right hand now, a scar runs down the center of the hand to the forearm. Three smaller scars adorn the hand, signs of other procedures to remove pins. The hand has been marked forever, and those marks are signs of both injury and healing. Those scars remind me that this body is a locus of healing activity, despite the fact of its mortality. There is a mystery here—the mystery of our very existence, the odd fact that we humans inhabit this earthly space for a short time.

The fact is that our bodies awaken us to this truth: we are not the sole authors of our existence. Every moment, every day, we live and move and have our being within this physical abode. That dwelling is continually being created, continually being healed, continually being renewed, until our mortal days come to an end. When we begin to receive our bodies as gift, our relationship to them shifts. We begin to see them. We begin to behold them as the place "wherein the Holy Spirit makes his dwelling."

Abiding Gratefulness

When a state of gratefulness begins to take hold, our habit of ignoring our bodies shifts. With kindly attention comes a deepening capacity for care and compassion. A friend of mine who is in her seventies has made a daily practice in the last decade of daily thanking her body for continuing to function, and thanking God for the resilience of her own temple of the Holy Spirit. She has found that this practice allows her to be more attentive to how she eats, how she exercises, how she rests—not out of sense of duty, but out of a sense of tenderness for her body. Furthermore, that tenderness has, in time, extended to others to the point that she now finds herself drawn to working as a hospital volunteer.

Gratefulness is so often engendered in the aftermath of loss. As in the case of my hand and wrist, the loss of function made me acutely aware of what I had not noticed. Growing in gratefulness is a way of being. Brother David Steindl-Rast has pointed out that gratefulness leads us to recognize "everything is gratuitous, everything is gift. The degree to which we are awake to this truth is the measure of our gratefulness. And gratefulness is the measure of our aliveness."[4]

For those of us in the Christian tradition, our regular participation in the eucharist reminds us of the centrality of gratefulness. The Greek word "eucharist" means "thanksgiving." When we celebrate it, we come together around Christ's table, to receive the sacrament of communion, the bread and the wine. We recognize in the liturgy that we offer ourselves in the bread and the wine, and we receive "the gifts of God for the people of God" as we partake of the food and drink. We are reminded that our lives are gifts from God, and we are formed by a way of gratefulness or thanksgiving. Clearly, gratefulness is foundational to our spiritual lives.

When we allow this sense of gratitude to stir within us, and are thankful for the daily miracle of opening our eyes, breathing deeply, beholding the faces of those we love, we begin to quicken in body and spirit. The deep numbness caused by too much of too much—food, possessions, activity, work, drugs—begins to wear off.

From Numbness to Gratitude

As when anesthesia begins to wear off after a dental procedure, there is a kind of "tingling" that occurs as our spiritual awareness is restored. When we are in the dental chair and receive an anesthetic, its numbing effect protects us from pain. That said, no doubt you are aware of that disconcerting sensation of not being able to feel your lip or cheek once the dental cavity is filled and you are getting into your car. The tingling that signals the departure of the anesthetic from our mouth also tells us that the sensory abilities of those nerves are returning. In an analogous way, as our spiritual numbness wears off, we may feel a kind of quickening as we develop eyes to see and ears to hear. Our spiritual "nerves" begin functioning, and we see anew that everything is gift, freely offered, freely bestowed. Because of gratefulness, we find ourselves grounded in hope. The Giver of the gift of life is truly with us at every moment, weaving together new cells, supporting metabolic processes. We are more able to hold the paradox that the body is a wonder, and the body is a finite creation. We are less inclined to fall into the sickness of entitlement.

Author Wilkie Au has pointed out that in our culture, entitlement is encouraged rather than gratitude. As long as we are in the throes of feeling entitled, we live in a kind of slavery. As he observes, "When we feel entitled to everything, we end up thankful for nothing."[5] Au discerns several ways in which a sense of entitlement cripples us spiritually:

- an inability to admit shortcoming and limitations,
- feelings of envy and resentment,
- overemphasis on materialistic values, and
- perceptions of being a victim.

This becomes evident very quickly with regard to the body. When I feel entitled, it leads me to assume that I should not have to live with any limitations whatsoever. Consequently, as I age, I might be tempted to keep acting as if I were in my forties instead of my sixties. If I have some kind of physical limitation, either temporary or permanent, I might push too hard and make the situation worse. When I live from an assumption of entitlement, I completely miss the gifted nature of life itself. To make things worse, in health care settings I may assume I am at the center of everything and entitled to the physician's full attention when, in fact, my condition is hardly critical. So I may resent not being given an appointment at my preferred time. I may be unwilling to take responsibility for my own role in my health and wellbeing, and insist that any difficulties I experience are directly due to the shortcomings of doctors, therapists, nurses or technicians. Believing in our own entitlement is like putting on blinders—we fail to see ourselves as part of a larger whole, and we fail to see the gift of the body itself.

Once we stop, reflect, and recognize our physicality, however, something new can begin. When I first became ill from acute pancreatitis, and the doctor had just given me the diagnosis in the emergency room, my first question was, "Where is my pancreas?" I did not have any awareness whatsoever of that organ. I certainly did not know anything about the metabolic processes that occur within the pancreas, nor did I have any idea that the malfunction of the pancreas could cause so much distress and pain.

Each of us has been given a body, has been gifted with physical life on this planet. No matter how tall or short you are, no matter your eye color or skin color, no matter how old or how young you are—your body is not of your making. Your body is a primary gift. The reality of your body's ability to function, to transform, to metabolize, to heal is a reality that this book invites you to embrace.

PART 2

The Meditations

In the following chapters, you will find meditations on some of the organs of the body. They contain information about how the organ works, where it is located and how it interacts with other organs as well as material from poetry and fiction. I have not tried to address every organ and system in the body. This is not an anatomy textbook, but a beginner's guide to remembering the gift of the body.

Take the time to read each meditation slowly and use it to allow yourself to become acquainted with your body. This portion of the book is not meant to be read quickly. You may find that you are best served by putting it down for awhile, and then returning to it after you have had some days or weeks to pray and reflect. You may discover that as you learn about a particular organ or function of the body, you want to know more about that organ or function, rather than continuing to the next meditation. As with any contemplative practice, if you discover that one meditation has become a "way station" in your journey through the text, allow yourself to rest at that place and to receive the insights being offered in your own prayer and meditation. You may find it helpful to have a journal in which to record your responses, questions, discoveries and prayers.

At the end of each chapter there is a short final prayer, followed by a sequence of suggested practices. If you find that none of the practices speak to you, there is no need to force yourself to do them. If you prefer to do one practice rather than all, please do so. In short, take what speaks to you and leave the rest.

For some readers, it will be helpful to have a visual aid. For good online images of human anatomy, I recommend *www.nlm.nih.gov/medlineplus/anatomy.html*. This is a site that is created and updated through the National Institute of Health. It also has links to other resources. The website of National Geographic offers some good interactive images for organs of the body as well: *science.national geographic.com/science/health-and-human-body/human-body/*. You can, for example, click on an image of the layers of the skin, and see how the body heals from a shallow cut or a deep cut. Also, there are apps available for tablets such as iPad, although some of them require the latest versions and are not free.

3

The Heart

We often speak of the heart in powerful ways, with phrases like "my heart aches for you," or "I'm holding you in my heart," or "her heart is broken." This complex and amazing physical organ works powerfully in our symbolic and our everyday speech, yet we often take its daily work for granted until something goes wrong. Day after day, hour after hour, minute after minute, the heart beats within the chest. And that beat, that continual lub-dub, is essential for life. That rhythm of the heart is the heart of life.

A friend of mine had a heart catheterization (a diagnostic procedure in which a thin, flexible tube is inserted into the coronary arteries to check for blockage and disease) and a subsequent angioplasty, in which the arteries of the heart are widened via a balloon catheter. In the aftermath of the procedure and of the recovery period, Joe began to reflect on the singular marvel that is his heart. One day when I went to visit him, he was making calculations at his desk. When I asked him what he was doing, he replied, "I am trying to figure out, more or less, how many times my heart has beaten in my life time. I keep thinking of all of the days and nights that it has kept its steady rhythm, without my attention or care. I keep thinking that I have really taken this for granted." Joe was beginning to understand that the quiet, steady rhythm of the human heart beats in the depths of human life and culture. Without the heart, and without its ability to push the blood from veins to arteries, through the lungs and out through the vast network of capillaries, we simply cannot exist.

The heart works (as do all of our organs) every moment of our lives, whether we are aware of it or not. The heart is a muscle, an extraordinary muscle with exquisite timing which, when disrupted, causes grave problems. Brian Doyle, a writer whose son's heart had congenital malformation, writes, "It weighs eleven ounces. It feeds a vascular system that comprises sixty thousand miles of veins and arteries and capillaries. It beats a hundred thousand times a day. It shoves two thousand gallons of blood through the body every day. It begins when a fetus is three weeks old and a cluster of cells begins to pulse with the cadence of that particular person, a music and a rhythm and a pace that will endure a whole lifetime. No one knows why the cluster of cells begins to pulse at that time or with that beat."[6]

When we stop to become aware of the wonder of the heart, we come to the mystery of life. How is it that the cluster of cells within the fetus begins to pulse when it does? How is it that the cells then begin to differentiate, and over a period of weeks, become a beating little heart? How is it that this "wet engine," to use Doyle's phrase, works day in and day out, most of the time without our attention?

The heart is about the size of a clenched fist, and located left of mid-point in the upper chest, between the lungs. Made up of four chambers, the heart both receives blood from the pulmonary veins and the vena cava (a very large vein that brings deoxygenated blood from the head and upper body), and pumps blood out to the pulmonary artery and the aorta. Clearly the heart and the lungs are intimately connected. The lower chambers of the heart, the ventricles, are thicker and more muscular than the upper chambers (the atria). The heart muscle needs continual oxygen and energy to do the work of regularly pumping blood throughout the body. When oxygen consumption is compromised, the heart cannot function properly. Similarly, when the body's energy is compromised, as with diabetic fluctuations, this will cause difficulties for the heart and the vascular system.

Shaped somewhat like a pear, the heart maintains a steady beat when it is working well. The rhythm that we notice in our pulse reflects the heart's regular beating, and the pumping of the blood in a double circulation—through the lungs in order to release carbon dioxide and pick up oxygen, and through the whole body, down to the smallest capillaries.

Because the heart is working so hard and so continually, it has its own system of blood supply called "coronary arteries." These bring needed nutrients and oxygen to the heart muscle itself. In addition, coronary veins transport the blood that is removing waste products from the heart itself. This complex rhythm is maintained throughout our waking and our sleeping. When it is disrupted, severe consequences ensue, sometimes resulting in death.

Our intrinsic adult heartbeat is usually around a hundred beats per minute. If we exercise or if we become stressed, frightened, excited or anxious, that beat will speed up; when asleep, it slows down. Electrochemical signals from the brain, sent along nerve pathways, alter the rate at which our heart beats. If you are someone who meditates regularly or practices centering prayer, you are perhaps aware that those habits have the physiological effect of slowing your heart and allowing it to rest, and it may even lower your blood pressure. Breath, heartbeat, the central nervous system, and our circulatory systems are all beneficially aided by meditation and quiet prayer, by walking meditation (such as a labyrinth), and by regular rest.

An older friend of mine has had to have a pacemaker placed in his chest in order to regulate the rhythm of his heart. As Tom has progressed through the round of diagnostic procedures and various consultations with cardiologists, he has become more and more awestruck by the electrical charges that keep the heart going. "Within my own chest," he observed, "something of the mystery of God's presence dwells. I did not manage the timing of those beats during the time when my heart was working well. I took it all for granted. I never paid it a whit of attention. And now that the beating needs some support, I am full of wonder that any heart ever beats in rhythm. How is that possible?"

Sometimes the disruption of health directs us toward this path of wonder and awe. Sometimes, after the initial shock of the onset of illness, we are led to have eyes to see and ears to hear. When our lives are shaken to the core by illness, the shaking that makes us anxious and afraid may also be the very thing that wakes us from spiritual blindness and deafness. That awakening leads us to notice "the wonder of life, the mystery of love" (BCP 836).

Gracious God, you knit me together in my mother's womb. I thank you for my heart, for all the minutes, days, hours that it has beat within me. I thank you for the marvel of its structure, and for the wonder of its work. I remember this day all whose hearts labor from malfunction and disease, and give thanks for those who tend them. Amen.

Practices

1. Sitting in a comfortable position (or lying comfortably if needed), place your hands very gently over your heart. Breathe slowly and steadily, allowing yourself to become aware of the beating of your heart. Let your hands feel the singular rhythm of your heart. Begin to pray, "Thank you" in rhythm with the heartbeat. Stay with this prayer as long as you wish.

2. Sitting or lying in a comfortable position, close your eyes and bring your attention to your breath. Gently allow the

inhalation to deepen, and exhale slowly. After breathing in this way for five to ten minutes, imagine your breath bathing the heart, inside and out. And with the breath, receive God's Spirit of love, enfolding your physical heart, no matter what condition it is in. End the prayer with an expression of thanks.

3. For this practice you will need paper and colored markers or crayons. Draw a picture of your heart. This does not need to be anatomically correct. The picture is a way for you to be aware of your heart, and to "see" the way that you are becoming aware of it. Take your time, and try not to let yourself be critical of the drawing. This is a form of prayer in and of itself. (The first time I did this, the heart I drew was blue. Then I reflected on that particular color as well.) When the drawing is finished, put it where you will see it daily, as a reminder to give thanks for your heart, and to tend to its health.

4. Do an online search for "images of the human heart." Pick one and allow yourself to attend to the complexity and detail of the heart. Return to the image from time to time. What do you notice when you see the image of the heart anew? Print out the image for further meditation.

5. Taking the picture of the heart that you have drawn in practice 3, and the image of the anatomical rendering of the heart that you have printed out in 4, begin a simple collage. Use these two images of the heart, adding phrases, pictures, photographs—whatever seems to be right for this collage. Allow the creation of the collage to be a way of becoming acquainted with the wonder of your own heart, and a prayer of thanksgiving.

4

The Lungs

Every day, at every moment, our lungs are quietly working. In an intricately designed pattern, our inhalations and exhalations allow us to be among the living. Taken together, the two lungs are one of the largest organs in the body. Often described in anatomy books as "spongy," the lungs inhabit our upper chest, just inside the ribcage. The right lung is slightly larger than the left, due to the placement of the heart.

When we breathe in, air passes from the nose (and sometimes the mouth) down the trachea, into the bronchial passages on each side, and eventually to tiny sacs called alveoli. In those alveoli an efficient and amazing transfer takes place as oxygen is taken up by red blood cells (hemoglobin cells) and carbon dioxide is offloaded. Moreover, "the tissue surface area involved in this exchange is about 40 times greater than the body's outer surface."[7] In other words, the total surface area of these tiny grape-like sacs called alveoli is extensive. Within our chests, within the lungs themselves, these alveoli are the place of transformation and exchange, working continually every moment of our lives.

When we breathe out, the lungs expel the carbon dioxide into the air, and then the cycle begins again. We see the process known as "external respiration"—that rhythm of inhalation and exhalation that tells us that life is present. Beyond our sight, on the cellular level, the process of "internal respiration" occurs. At that microscopic level, the hemoglobin that departed from the lungs laden with oxygen then carries that oxygen to the cells, and picks up the carbon dioxide. The hemoglobin then begins its return journey to the lungs, carrying with it the waste gas created by cellular metabolism.

The patterns of external and internal inhalation are with us every moment of our lives. Without them we would not be alive. These patterns, on both the visible level and the cellular level, allow the body to receive the oxygen essential for life, and to expel the waste gas of carbon dioxide. With each breath in, each breath out, the body is both enlivened and cleansed. With each breath in, each breath out, the body is renewed.

We cannot *not* breathe. Try holding your breath for as long as you can: sooner or later you have to let go and breathe in. Our breathing is under the control of the autonomic nerve system, which is in the brainstem. Even when we try to hold our breath, the autonomic nerve system will override our attempt, and we will have to take a breath. On average, at rest we breathe twelve to fifteen times per minute. That means that the lungs make at least 17,000 cycles of inhalation and exhalation per day and around 6 million a year. With every one of those breaths, the respiratory system warms incoming air, filters it and humidifies it.

As you know, emotions can also change the rate of our breathing. Perhaps you have had the experience of hyperventilating (breathing too fast) when anxious or stunned by terrible news, or by something that brings overwhelming joy. Sensors in the brain, blood vessels, muscles and lungs all help alter the rate of breathing in response to circumstance and environment.

By now I hope I have shown you that the work and the anatomy of the lungs is intricate and amazing. The interdependence of the organs of the body is also clear—the lungs and the respiratory system are intimately connected to the heart and the circulatory system, the brain, the muscles, the rib cage and to every cell. We begin to be aware of the ways in which one aspect of organ health or disease can affect the whole of the body. We also begin to notice the body's extraordinary design.

From the scriptural perspective, these lungs of ours also receive the breath of the Holy Spirit, which animates the body. In the account of creation given in the second chapter of Genesis, we read, "Then the LORD God formed man from the dust of the ground, and breathed into his nostrils the breath of life; and the man [*adam*] became a living being" (Gen. 2:7). As biblical scholar Walter Brueggemann has remarked in his commentary on Genesis, *adam* is an androgynous being formed of the dust—*adamah*. Matter and divine breath are compatible from the beginning. This breath of life swells the lungs, charges the blood with oxygen, animates every limb and organ.

Adam, the earth-creature, begins to take breath, and that act of breathing signals both utter dependence upon the living God and intimate kinship to God. When we allow ourselves to pay attention to our breath, to our lungs, to the miracle of both outer and inner respiration, we are reacquainted with our own beginnings—at birth, at dawn, at each event that life throws at us. We are invited to remember that we share breath with all that breathes. We are, in fact, breathed into being by the Holy One. We are sustained and recreated by breath at every instant. Our lungs and respiratory systems are the means by which our earthly breath, inspirited and inspiriting, reminds us that we are creatures, and God is God.

~

Gracious and creating God, You breathe in me at every moment. You breathe the whole creation into being. Guide me in discovering the sacredness of your own breath in every being on this earth. As I reflect on my lungs and on the rhythms of inhalation and exhalation, may I be aware of those who struggle for breath, those who need respiratory therapy, and those medical personnel whose skill helps others breathe. Amen.

Practices

1. While sitting comfortably, either in a chair with your feet on the floor or on the floor with your back against the wall, begin by gently paying attention to your breath. With the inhalation, notice the expansion of your chest. With each inhalation, notice the inner shifts of lung, muscle, rib cage. As the breath settles into its own easy rhythm, add this breath prayer: "Breathe" (inhalation) . . . "in me" (exhalation). Allow the breath to breathe you. Pray in this way for five to ten minutes at first, and as you return to this practice from time to time, gradually lengthen the amount of time until you are spending twenty minutes a day with this prayer. As you dwell with this prayer, you may want to journal about attending to the experience of your lungs and body being refreshed and cleansed through breathing. You may want to note shifts in awareness and difficulties you might encounter.

2. Call to mind a time when you could not breathe easily. This could be something as ordinary as your last cold, or it could be something as acute as a bad case of bronchitis. Remember how it felt to have to work just to take a breath, and what it took for your body to acquire sufficient oxygen. If you have been placed on oxygen therapy at some point in your life, allow yourself to remember the sensation of the plastic prongs in your nostrils, the whispers of the oxygen tank, the feeling of being dependent upon an external source of oxygen.

   Now shift your attention to those who struggle to breathe but do not have access to medicines, physicians, or breathing equipment. Offer a prayer of intercession for those for whom breathing is a struggle. As you breathe, imagine breathing on their behalf and for their wellbeing. Next, become aware of the earth as a breathing whole. Allow your imagination to perceive the exchange of oxygen and carbon dioxide throughout the entire planet. Call to mind those cities and environments that are plagued by polluted air. Spend some time breathing rhythmically, becoming aware of the essential need for oxygen and clean air.

Finally, if you are so led by this reflection, connect with a local or national organization that supports efforts to create cleaner environments.

3. In Hebrew, the word for "breath" is *ruach*, which also means "spirit," while in Greek the word *pneuma* carries both of these meanings. Wind, breath, and spirit are interwoven and connected in the scriptural story. As you begin to reflect on this, draw a simple outline or diagram of your upper body and your lungs. You may want to use a big sheet of construction paper or, alternatively, you may want to print out an anatomical image from the Internet and use that as the basis for the next step.

Once you have made the preliminary sketch or chosen an online image, then sit quietly, noticing the rhythm of your breath. As you attend to your breathing, reflect on the word "spirit." Remember that the inner respiration reaches each of your cells. Let your imagination follow the breath as a vehicle of God's own Spirit, seeking out every cell in your body. Then imagine the return of the breath to the lungs and the ensuing exhalation. Stay with this portion of the meditation as long as you wish.

Then return to your preliminary sketch. Using paint, colored marker or pastels—whatever medium you choose—create an image of your lungs filled with God's Spirit. Spend some time with the image once you have finished. Then place your drawing in a place where you can see it regularly, so that it can remind you of the sacred work of the lungs.

5

The Liver

In his novel about the lives of two young surgeons, *Cutting for Stone*, Abraham Verghese, himself a surgeon, writes, "If the beating heart is pure theater, a playful, moody, extroverted organ cavorting in the chest, then the liver, sitting under the diaphragm, is a figurative painting, stolid and silent."[8] We began this series of meditations with the heart and the lungs. Many of us, during our schooling, have had some degree of familiarity with these two organs—in biology class I had occasion to see human lungs, though these were diseased from smoking and therefore particularly unlovely. Since my grandfather was a physician, I had seen color photos of the heart in his medical books, spread out on the dining room table while he caught up on continuing education. But the liver? Many of us have not spent much time thinking about this organ.

In this novel Verghese gives us a surgeon's view of the liver: "The liver's smooth and shiny outer surface is monotonous and unexciting, and apart from a median furrow dividing it into a large right lobe and a smaller left, it has no visible cleavage planes."[9] One might expect, given these descriptions of the stolid, quiet presence of the liver, that not much is happening inside of it. Quite the contrary. Though appearing stolid and silent, the liver is sometimes compared to an engine. In adults, it is roughly the size of a football, weighing some three pounds. Situated on the right side of the body, the liver is tucked underneath the lower right rib cage and extends down beneath the diaphragm.

Many chemical transformations occur within the liver. It produces a digestive fluid called bile that breaks down fats into smaller molecules so that the body can readily use them. It produces cholesterol, which is needed in appropriate amounts for the creation of new cells and the maintenance of existing ones. In addition, the liver utilizes amino acids to make proteins and serves to store iron, glycogen, and vitamins. Furthermore, the liver detoxifies and cleanses the blood, removing poisons and waste products.

All of these transformations happen continually, without our conscious help. We can certainly make the work of the liver harder by consuming excessive amounts of alcohol and other substances. When I imagine the liver in my own body, I imagine an organ that quietly and steadily continues to transform chemicals, to provide energy and proteins and to cleanse the blood. All of these processes are happening at the same time. The liver has the capacity to "multi-task," so to speak, in a way that is essential to the body's health. More than *five hundred* vital functions have been identified with the liver.

It is remarkable for its regenerative capacity. We can lose up to three quarters of our liver and still survive, because it has an amazing ability to create new liver tissue from as little as one fourth of the original organ. If the portion of the liver that remains is healthy, those cells can create new cells, so that the organ will quite literally be made new.

All of the blood in the body flows through the liver after departing the stomach and intestines. The liver aids in blood clotting by creating clotting factors that help to stop bleeding in the event of a cut or an injury, and also removes harmful bacteria from the blood and cleanses it of impurities. In other words, the liver has an essential part to play in the health of our whole body. In cleansing the blood and creating clotting factors, the liver actually prepares the blood for its continual circulation from head to toe. The heart pumps the blood, the lungs oxygenate the blood and remove carbon dioxide, and the liver strengthens and cleanses the blood for its journey throughout the body.

In short, the liver is a true workhorse when it comes to cleansing and transformation. Though to a surgeon's eye, it may appear quiet and still, on a cellular level the liver is stunningly active and efficient. Vital processes—the ones that literally keep us alive and lively—occur in that large organ, tucked in our upper right abdomen. While we sleep, while we work, while we play, the liver filters the blood, stores needed elements for new cells, and participates in production of proteins. This organ called "liver" truly supports life.

⁓

God of all hopefulness and joy, I thank you for the work of my liver, for its varied functions that allow this body to be well-nourished with blood and nutrients. I thank you for the ways that my liver cleanses and heals, regenerates and restores the cells that pass through its vessels. May I remember its quiet, steady work as I go about my day. Just as the liver quietly goes about the work of transformation and cleansing, may I remember your transforming and cleansing presence throughout the whole earth. Amen.

Practices

1. Place your hands on the right side of your body, in the region of your lower rib cage. Your liver dwells in that space under your hands. Sit quietly, with your hands resting there gently. Breathe deeply, and with each breath imagine the breath bathing the liver. Imagine light coursing through the blood vessels of the liver, illumining that organ from within. Then, as you breathe, if you wish, add this breath prayer: "Gracious God" (inhalation) . . . "thank you" (exhalation).

2. Take a moment to look at an anatomical drawing of the liver from an online site such as WebMD (*www.webmd.com*),

or, if you desire something more precise, just type "anatomy of human liver" into your search engine. Once you
have found it, notice that the liver is situated at midpoint
in the trunk of the body. It is also nestled under the ribcage, and other organs (stomach, gall bladder, pancreas,
small intestine, lungs) are close at hand.

Allow yourself to gaze on the image of the liver, and
as you do so, place your hands gently on your right side
(as in practice 1 above). Spend a few moments imagining
your own liver, working steadily even as you pray. Close
with a simple prayer of thanksgiving.

3. In your journal, write down as accurately as you can what
you have had to eat and drink in the last twenty-four hours.
As you look over the list, notice the amount of alcohol and
the amount of fats consumed, because an overabundance
of either of these causes more work for the liver. If you
have been consuming more fat or alcohol than you think
is good for you, simply notice that and recognize the possibility of altering the amounts you ingest. Moderation will
befriend the liver! It allows this organ to work at a gentler
pace, enhancing the health of the whole body.

4. In the Hebrew Bible the liver is sometimes regarded
as the seat of feeling. Thus verse 9 of Psalm 16, usually
rendered "My heart, therefore, is glad and my spirit
rejoices" or "my soul rejoices," could also be translated as
"Therefore my heart is glad and my liver rejoices." Sitting
or lying quietly, begin offering this breath prayer: "My
liver" (inhalation) . . . "rejoices" (exhalation). As you
allow the prayer to find its own rhythm with your breath,
imagine the joy of your liver. How does that joy register
in your body? What might you imagine to be the visible
signs of a joyful liver? Allow yourself to be playful in your
response, and glad for the liver's contentment. Bring the
prayer gently to a close by placing your hands over your
right mid-torso, and giving thanks for all of the liver's
transformational processes.

6

The Pancreas

What comes to mind when you imagine the pancreas? Where is it in your body? What does the pancreas do? Poet Gretchen White, giving thanks for her healthy pancreas after an abominal ultrasound, wrote these words of praise:

Ode to My Pancreas
You make insulin.
For that, I humbly thank you.
I can eat some cake.

Herophilus was
The Greek guy who discovered you,
and then he ate you.

Don't know if *that's* true,
but some people in far places
eat you in sweetbread.

I'd rather love you.
I'd rather trumpet beauty,
found twixt moon-hued ribs.

Excrete on and on,
hormones and enzymes delight!
My body will sing.

Evermore favored,
Praised by those in scrubs and Crocs,
my self-esteem soared!

(I must wonder, though
what part of me is hungry
for strange approval?)

Endocrine's esteem!
Exocrine's favor increased!
Wondertwin powers!

Unite! Two functions,
one hardy, blessed organ:
Brava, pancreas.[10]

Not many of us have this kind of relationship with our pancreas! Most of us don't know where it is, and most of us don't know what it does, yet its role in our overall health and the body's ability to function cannot be overstated.

Hidden behind the stomach, the pancreas is a gland. If you clench your right hand, extending your ring finger and pinkie, and place it at the base of your sternum in the ribcage, you will have a sense of where the pancreas lies, and a notion of its size. Buried beneath the stomach, it lies close to the spine. Around six inches long, the pancreas is oblong in shape.

As Gretchen White points out in her poem, the pancreas creates both hormones and enzymes. Its exocrine function discharges digestive enzymes through the pancreatic duct, down into the common bile duct, into the part of the small intestine known as the duodenum. Its endocrine function secretes hormones into the bloodstream. These hormones (insulin and glucagon) regulate blood sugar. The pancreas is always doing both things at the same time. Like so many of our organs, a healthy pancreas is an amazing multi-processor. These two functions affect the life of the whole body. The hormonal system has a "global" effect on the body; since hormones travel via the bloodstream, they affect every part of the body. This gland serves us by regulating digestion and energy.

The enzymes that the pancreas excretes continue the process of the transforming of our food into proteins, carbohydrates, and fats, a process begun in our mouths and stomachs. The role of the pancreas is essential in allowing the body to absorb nutrients needed for the creation of new cells and for adequate energy to think, move, play, and work. If you stop and reflect on how essential sufficient energy is to the function of our brains, our internal organs and our muscles, you begin to have a sense of the importance of the pancreas. Recall for a moment the last time your own blood sugar ran low, and your thinking got fuzzy or your muscles felt weak. Utilizing energy from our food, the pancreas plays a continual role in balancing and calibrating the sugars needed to allow us to think, move, focus, play, create, and plan.

When healthy, the pancreas produces these hormones and enzymes at the right times and in the right quantities. The body benefits from the delivery of these chemicals when they are needed. If something blocks a pancreatic duct (such as a gall stone), the enzymes will back up into the pancreas itself, creating terrible pain and inflammation (pancreatitis).

Too much fat, too much alcohol, and too much sugar in our diet can all contribute to difficulties with the pancreas. Moderation with regard to food and alcohol helps to keep it healthy. Awareness of this hard-working gland, tucked away in the core of the body, leads us to a deepening sense of the ways in which our lives are governed by these inner organs, working steadily and mysteriously, without our aid.

Gracious God, I thank you for the work of the pancreas, for its ability to balance blood sugar and its role in digestion. I thank you for the intricacies of its structure and the ways in which it regulates so many aspects of the body's health. May I be mindful of the pancreas, hidden within, and know it to be your own creation. Amen.

Practices

1. Write a short prayer giving thanks for your pancreas and its various functions, incorporating what you have learned in this chapter. End with, "I will thank you because I am marvelously made."

2. Place a hand gently on your upper abdomen, just at the base of the sternum. Breathing gently, allow yourself to imagine the pancreas, nestled behind the stomach and just in front of the spine. As you breathe, quietly thank God for the work of the pancreas and for its steady work of transformation. Allow yourself to imagine the insulin and glucagon entering your bloodstream and flowing throughout your whole body.

3. The pancreas plays an essential role in the balancing of blood sugar. As you read above, the pancreas releases regulatory hormones. It has an essential role in supplying energy needed by the body—energy for thinking, moving, reflecting, digesting, and all aspects of bodily life. If you have ever had a moment when you knew your blood sugar was far too low, you may have experienced forgetfulness or irritability. For most of us, these are passing moments readily corrected by a piece of fruit or a glass of juice. For others who suffer from diabetes, the delicate balance of blood sugar is an ongoing challenge and frustration.

   Pray attentively for all who suffer from diabetes in its various manifestations. Remember how difficult the management of this malady can be. Give thanks for your own pancreas as it handles the challenge of regulating blood sugar without disruption. If you know someone who lives with diabetes, pray for that particular person and for his or her physicians.

7

The Stomach

M y hunch is that we become consciously aware of our stomachs early on, even before we have language to speak about them. So much of the daily existence of a baby is focused on how the stomach is doing—she spends so much time eating, dealing with colic, burping, spitting up. Her stomach also adapts over time, moving from a liquid diet to a soft diet and then to solid food. That process of adaptation tells us that the stomach takes time to function happily in life outside the womb. Later on, little children often begin speaking of tummy aches. Clearly the work of adapting continues for a long time, sometimes into adulthood. A kindergartener will often have a clearer sense of having a stomach than of having lungs or even a heart. That is because the stomach of a five year old is still a work in progress, whereas, in general, the heart and the lungs do their job without a lot of adjusting and tending.

Our digestive systems are made up of a series of hollow, connected organs starting with the mouth and ending at the anus. When we eat, digestion begins in the mouth. As we chew, saliva begins the initial breakdown of food. This breakdown is necessary for the body to receive the nutrients from the food, and is continued in the stomach. From there the digestive process continues through the small intestine, the large intestine and the colon. The food's full journey usually takes from twenty-four to forty-eight hours. As it is transferred from one digestive organ to the next, both acid and enzymes mix with the food, making its essential components available for the body's use.

The walls of the stomach are made of strong muscles (as are those of the whole digestive tract). When we eat, muscular contractions called "peristalsis" move the food through the digestive tract. Like ocean waves, the contractions ripple through as the food is swallowed and broken down. While eating involves choice—opening our mouths, chewing and swallowing—after the food is swallowed the ensuing process occurs without our conscious involvement. Once the food descends through the esophagus, the valve at the top of the stomach opens to receive the food. Hydrochloric acid from the stomach and enzymes are mixed with the food by the muscular contractions of the stomach.

Only water, alcohol, and certain other liquids are absorbed by the body through the stomach, while everything else continues the journey into the small intestine. The stomach itself, situated to the left of center in the upper torso, expands to receive a meal. It's worth reflecting on the size of the stomach. Empty, the adult stomach is about the size of your fist, but it has the ability to expand to receive as much as four liters of food. Of course, that would cause some degree of discomfort. The more food the stomach receives at one time, the harder it has to work. Therefore, if you are someone who habitually struggles with eating too much, becoming familiar with the size of the stomach and with the labor entailed in digesting large amounts of food may help you find a more balanced approach to eating.

The stomach accomplishes three mechanical tasks:

- It stores swallowed food and liquid when the muscle in the upper part of the stomach relaxes to accept what has been swallowed.

- In the lower part it mixes food, liquid, and digestive juices.
- It slowly empties these contents into the duodenum, the first segment of the small intestine. Carbohydrates stay in the stomach for the least amount of time; protein takes longer to digest. Fats stay in the stomach for the greatest amount of time.

The hydrochloric acid of the stomach is so strong that if a drop of it were placed on a piece of wood, it would actually eat through it. For that reason the walls of the stomach are protected by an alkaline substance that neutralizes the acid, a bicarbonate solution that keeps the stomach from digesting itself. Clearly, the right balance of acid and alkaline substances is necessary for the health and well being of the stomach. As you may know, many people suffer with a condition called "acid reflux," which is caused when the acids in the stomach back up into the esophagus—a classic case of disturbance caused when something is not where it is supposed to be!

Creator of all cells, of all bodies, I thank you for my stomach. I thank you for its ability to digest food. I thank you for its ability to expand and contract, and for its key role in the process of converting food and liquid into nutrients for my body. May I be mindful of ways in which gentle patterns of eating will cause my stomach less stress, and may I remember that in honoring the work of my stomach, I honor you as its creator. Amen.

Practices

1. Sitting quietly, imagine your stomach to the left of center, in your mid-torso. Hold your fist in this general area. This will give you a sense of the size of your stomach when it is empty. Now imagine the amount of food that you consumed at your last meal. Open your fist, imagining that the fist is accommodating that amount of food. Reflect on the

amount of digesting that your stomach accomplished with that one meal. Then, create a prayer giving thanks for your stomach and the task of digestion that it accomplishes.

2. Because we see so many television advertisements for medications to diminish stomach acid, we have often seen "talking stomachs" or "walking stomachs" in those advertisements. In some ways, these kinds of images affect the way we regard our own stomachs. Spend some time looking at anatomical drawings of the stomach online; you can find them by searching for "anatomy of the human stomach." As you behold these images, allow yourself to become aware of your own stomach. Reflect on its ability to adapt, expand, contract, and digest. Consider how you can foster the ongoing health of your stomach, and write down at least three ways in which you can honor the life of your hard-working stomach. These could be as simple as "I will eat smaller meals" or "I will stop drinking carbonated sodas." This is a practice of befriending the stomach and the body.

3. We use "stomach" as a verb in the English language. For example, I might say, "I just can't stomach the way he uses violent imagery." Or I might speak figuratively: "That rhetoric hurts my stomach." What do you find difficult to stomach? How might attending to the physical response of your stomach help you be aware of your own deep responses? Sometimes our stomachs clench in response to overwhelming life events, such as the death of someone important to us. At other times excessive stress will register as an awareness of a stomach that is never truly hungry.

Begin noticing what your stomach tells you, and gently allow yourself to be mindful of the stomach's "language" and cues. Note these over time, giving thanks for the ways in which your stomach gives you information that your other senses may not be picking up as readily.

8

The Kidneys

When I was growing up, my Czech physician grandfather would invite me to eat both beef liver and kidneys. He came from peasant stock and was accustomed to organ meats, but the aroma that filled the kitchen when my grandmother was preparing kidneys was not one that I found appetizing. It reminded me of the bathroom, and with good reason. Our kidneys produce urine, and that urine flows out of the body through the bladder. Kidneys work to keep the body cleansed of waste products in blood and of toxins. However, I've discovered that they also do a wide variety of other beneficial tasks for the whole body.

We have two bean-shaped kidneys, one on either side of the spine, at the middle of the back, just below the rib cage. As you may know, we can function, and function pretty well, with just one kidney. We've been provided with some abundance in this regard, which allows those who have kidney ailments to survive with one of them.

The website of the National Institute of Health describes the kidneys in this way: "The kidneys are sophisticated reprocessing machines. Every day, a person's kidneys process about 200 quarts of blood to sift out about two quarts of waste products and extra water."[11] The kidneys remove matter that results from the normal breakdown of muscle and of food. Were these waste products to remain in the blood, a toxic state would quickly ensue, endangering the health of the whole body. The regular filtering and cleansing of the blood accomplished by the kidneys is essential to the overall well-being of the body.

The process of waste removal is accomplished in tiny parts of the kidneys called "nephrons." Each kidney has about a million of these. Within the nephron, a tiny sieve called a "glomerulus" keeps healthy proteins and cells in the bloodstream, while also allowing waste to pass out of the blood. In addition, an intricate chemical exchange occurs during this process, an exchange by which the kidneys balance the pH of the body. The kidneys are agents of "right balance" within the body, releasing chemicals like sodium, phosphorus, and potassium as needed to maintain the body's optimal chemical makeup. Salt, potassium, and acid are all regulated by the kidneys. At the same time, they produce hormones that affect other organs (for example, one hormone stimulates the production of red blood cells).

As well as producing urine, the kidneys also perform a variety of other essential functions. They

- remove waste products from the body,
- remove drugs from the body,
- balance the body's fluids,
- release hormones that help regulate blood pressure,
- produce an active form of vitamin D that promotes strong bones, and
- control the production of red blood cells.

In short, these small, often overlooked organs, have much to do with the overall health of our bodies. Healthy kidneys need plenty of hydration. Their work is enhanced by moderation in eating and drinking alcohol, by moderate exercise, and by not smoking. If you are at risk for diabetes, it would be wise to have your glucose levels checked regularly; some diabetics develop kidney failure.

My mother, who lived with type 2 diabetes for some years, eventually died of end-stage renal failure. She was on dialysis for two years before her life came to an end. and as a dialysis patient, her blood was completely "washed" by a dialysis machine every other day. The dialysis treatment often lasted several hours, after which she would be exhausted. I often thought, beholding the dialysis machine, that although on the one hand I was grateful that the work of the machine could extend her life, on the other I was saddened that a big machine had to replicate the work of my mother's kidneys, along with a variety of shots and supplements. In other words, what the kidneys accomplished naturally could be replicated mechanically, but not with the delicate symmetry and efficiency of the organs themselves. My mother's experience taught me to respect the work of our kidneys, and to be grateful for their role in overall health.

For my kidneys, O creator God, I give you thanks—for their work of filtration, of cleansing, of maintaining chemical balances in the body. I remember their role in creating red blood cells and their ability to create an active form of vitamin D. I pray for those who live with kidney disease, and for those who await kidney transplant. For all of the ways in which my kidneys keep my body sound and healthy, I praise you and thank you, O Lord. Amen.

Practices

1. Sitting quietly, imagine your kidneys on either side of your spine, just above your waist level, and just below the base of your ribcage. Try to visualize them within your torso, continually receiving blood for filtering, for balancing chemicals, and for receiving hormones. As you sit quietly, direct the breath to the kidneys. If you are able, bring the palms of your hands to rest gently over the part of your back beneath which they rest. For a few minutes, breathe

gently, hands in place, offering the phrase "thank You, thank You," in rhythm with the breath. When you sense that the prayer has been completed, write a short prayer of thanksgiving for your kidneys in your journal.

2. Pour yourself a glass of water, giving thanks for the ready access to clean water. Then take a sip of the water, allowing your imagination to follow its course down through your esophagus to your stomach. From there, it will be absorbed and, after being used in the body, will make its way to your kidneys. Once processed by the kidneys, the water will make its way out through the bladder and the urethra. Yes, this is the bodily process of elimination—a process we tend to find not worth our attention until something goes wrong. Give thanks for your kidneys and bladder. Give thanks for this physical reality and for the coursing of the water throughout your body and then into the sewer system.

3. Sitting still and quietly breathing, allow yourself to imagine your kidneys. Recall all of the various metabolic processes that are occurring within them as you sit quietly. Remember their ability to cleanse the blood, to keep the body in chemical balance, and to participate in the creation of blood cells. Then as you imagine the kidneys being gently bathed in light, pray silently: "The wonder of life, the mystery of love."

4. In the Hebrew scriptures, the kidneys are perceived to be organs that reveal the truth of a person's soul before God.[12] The Hebrew word *kelayot*, the plural noun for "kidneys," tends to be translated in contemporary English as "mind" or "soul." However, since the original Hebrew refers to the actual organs, for this practice reflect on Psalm 26:2, for which the Hebrew could be rendered, "Test me, O Lord, and try me; examine my heart and my kidneys." We tend to use this language only figuratively. Allow yourself to imagine what your kidneys would reveal about how you honor the body you have been given, and how you honor the bodies of others.

9

The Skin

O ur skin, what poet Philip Larkin calls our "obedient daily dress,"[13] is the largest of all of our organs and probably the least appreciated. Every day we wash our skin and cover much of it with clothing. Every day we behold it in a mirror, or as we dress. Yet most of the time, our skin is not on our "radar"—until we cut it or burn it or bruise it, or it starts to wrinkle.

Were it laid out in a sheet, the skin of an average adult would cover between twenty and twenty-two square feet, which is probably much more than you would have guessed. Our skin varies in thickness. It is thickest on the soles of our feet, and thinnest around our eyes. Made up of three layers, the skin holds everything within the body in an insulating shield. If we had no skin, all of our moisture would evaporate, and we would not be able to exist.

Our skin protects us from extreme heat and cold by helping to keep our body temperature regular. It also serves us by screening out harmful bacteria and chemicals. The manufacture of Vitamin D, so essential for strong bones, is in part the job of the skin. Throughout our skin, nerves also relay sensations of touch, temperature, weight, and texture to the brain, orienting us to our physical environment. The skin is phenomenally flexible, giving us the gift of freedom of movement because of its capacity to stretch and adapt.

The top layer of the skin, the epidermis, is made up of tough cells that are created from the protein keratin, which is also the material found in our hair and nails. These cells, known as keratinocytes, grow in several layers. They are constantly in the process of rising from the deeper layer of the epidermis to the top layer. We shed the cells of that outermost layer all of the time; every minute of every day we lose between thirty and forty thousand dead skin cells from the surface of our skin. Over the course of a year, we shed approximately nine pounds (four kilograms) of skin cells. Thus within a time span of about five weeks, you will have brand new cells on the surface of your skin, cells that were formed at the lower level of the epidermis and then worked their way to the surface. The skin, as you can see, is an outward and visible sign of our continually being made new. Without our attention or our influence, the epidermis is renewed continually.

The epidermis is also home to Langherhans cells, which are instrumental in alerting the body's immune system to the presence of viruses or other agents of infection. The skin is our first line of defense, and it serves to shield us from infection, injury to internal organs, and the harsh effects of weather.

The second layer of the skin, the dermis, is made up of fibers of collagen and elastin, which are different kinds of connective tissue. This second layer allows our skin to be elastic and flexible. In addition, within the dermis there are tiny blood vessels that help to regulate our body temperature. As warm-blooded creatures, optimally, our body temperature needs to be around 98.6 degrees. The skin helps in maintaining that temperature by insulating us from cold and heat. Within this second layer of skin, moreover, nerve receptors that communicate with the brain work all the time to provide information about what we are touching. Usually beyond the purview of our conscious attention, our brains are continually receiving signals from the skin that orient us to our immediate physical surroundings. The same nerves alert us to danger, such as heat from an open flame.

You have no doubt noticed that at times the hairs on your skin will stand up in response to cold or perhaps to fright. The follicles that control those hairs exist in the dermis, as do the sweat glands. Sweat allows the body to cool itself when needed, in heat or in physical exertion. In sweat the body also releases some waste chemicals through the pores of the skin. In this way, the skin functions as one of the various organs involved in detoxification of the body.

The last of these three layers of skin, the subcutis, is for the storage of fat. These fat-storage cells are called fibroblasts, adipocytes, and macrophages. The fat they conserve may be used as fuel when food is scarce—but if it isn't used, it will simply accumulate. This fat layer also helps to protect us from injury and to regulate our body temperature.

Finally, the color of our skin is determined by melanin, a pigment found in the epidermis. The more melanin our skin has, the darker it will be. Melanin protects us from the sun's ultraviolet rays, which can cause skin cancer.

~~~~~~

Creator of all the cells in my body, I thank you for the gift of my skin. I thank you for its ability to be made new. I thank you for the ways it protects me, insulates me, and shields me. May I remember to tend this skin as your own creation, and respect its dignity as your handiwork. Amen.

Practices

1. Find a comfortable position, either sitting or lying down. Allow yourself to pay attention to your breath, noticing the way the inhalation and exhalation feel on the skin at the base of your nostrils. Then, as you slowly breathe, allow yourself to feel the expansion and contraction of the skin of your upper torso as the breath's rhythm settles. Notice

the way the skin adapts to the expansion and contraction of your lungs. Then take time to notice the skin on your chest, on your sides, and in your back. As you become more deeply aware of the skin's elasticity and flexibility, form a simple prayer of thanks for its essential role in the health of your body.

2. Begin this practice by taking off your shoes and socks. Stand up or else sit in a chair with the soles of your feet on the floor. Slowly press each toe into the floor, one by one. Then notice the skin of the heel touching the floor. See if you can become aware of the space of the arch of your foot (for most of us, this will not touch the floor, so the sensation will be different than that of the heel or the toes). Pay attention to the way the skin feels—what is it telling you about the texture upon which you are standing? About the temperature? About fatigue of your feet or the rest of your body? About how your body is balanced? Try to spread your toes and then gently flex them. Then let them relax. What do you notice about the skin's abilities in your feet? Stand or sit quietly, breathing gently, noticing the skin on the soles of your feet, and giving thanks for the work of this thickest skin of your body.

3. Your skin is constantly protecting your body, insulating your body and cushioning your body. After your next bath or shower, when you apply moisturizer or lotion, apply it as a prayer of anointing. Apply the lotion with gratefulness and kindness for the skin that labors constantly, giving thanks for its role in your overall wellbeing. Pay attention to the sensation of the lotion as it is absorbed. When you are finished, stand or sit quietly, attending to the skin's resilience and texture. End with a short prayer of thanksgiving.

4. Many people suffer from a variety of ailments of the skin, everything from dermatitis to psoriasis to melanoma. If you have suffered from some kind of malady of the skin, or if you are close to someone who does, sit quietly and

remember all those around the world who also suffer from such ailments. Remember those whose skin has become disfigured or blotched. Pray for those who have little or no resources for care of their skin, and give thanks for the resources that you have.

5. Psalm 102 has given us this verse, "Because of the voice of my groaning/I am but skin and bones" (v. 5). Often the condition of a person's skin will readily indicate general health or illness to an examining nurse or physician. Pause to remember those whose lack of food or whose course of illness has led them to be "but skin and bones." If you have known a time of being "but skin and bones," give thanks for ongoing life.

10

The Bones

When I was in high school, I broke a bone in my foot one Fourth of July. We were setting off firecrackers in the backyard, and in jumping away from one while barefoot, I came down wrong and heard a little "pop." The next day, I looked at the x-ray of my foot. On the one hand, I was distressed to see the clearly broken bone (it was the outermost bone of the foot). On the other hand, I was amazed to see all of those bones—so many pieces fitting together into a larger whole. My family physician answered my questions about the bones, and pointed out all of the joints in the foot.

Later, when the doctor removed my cast, the foot was x-rayed again. We discovered that the bone had not healed well. There was a small hole in the middle of the repair, a hole where there should have been bone, which looked a little like a "Y." It took a long time for a calcification process to occur and for the little hole that had formed to be filled in. This meant that I had occasion to see x-rays of the bones of my foot with some regularity, and to watch for the slowly forming new bone. But my body, over time, took care of the open space. New cells were created. The cells hardened and slowly the bone became sturdy again.

Many of us have had an experience of living with a broken bone. I am the oldest of four children, and all of us broke at least one over the course of our childhood and adolescence, recovering with the help of a variety of casts. All of us have full use of our limbs, though now there's some arthritis in our aging bodies. And we took for granted that our bones would set, that we would recover full use of the arm, elbow, foot, or leg that had been broken.

Like our skin, it is easy for us to take our bones for granted. We have a lot of them—206 in the adult skeleton, to be exact. They are arranged symmetrically along the central axis of the body. When we first look at a human skeleton, we notice that there is a distinct vertical line from the top of the skull to the bottom of the pelvis. This is the axial skeleton, so named because our bodies are aligned along that axis. The skull, or cranium, is made up of twenty-two smaller bones. Of these, only the jawbone, or "mandible," moves at will. The smallest bone of the body, the stirrup bone in the ear, is found in the cranium. About the size of a grain of rice, the stirrup bone is one of three small bones that transmit sound vibrations in the ear.

Moving downward, the next sequence of bones in this axis is the spine. We have thirty-three vertebrae in the spine; they provide shape for the torso and also protect the spinal cord from injury. If you recall media discussions about spinal cord injury in professional sports, you will begin to have a sense of how important the vertebrae are to the health of the spinal cord. The central nervous system of the spinal cord connects our brains to the nerves that run throughout the body. When all is well with the spine, the spinal cord functions well because the vertebrae shield it from harm.

On the front side of the axial spine is the sternum. Essential to the protection of the heart, lungs, and portions of major blood vessels, the sternum is also the bone to which most of our ribs attach. The rib cage is made up of twenty-four ribs, twelve on each side, and within these ribs our major organs are enclosed and shielded. Connected to this axis are the appendicular bones—the bones of our outer limbs. These include the bones of the shoulder, the arm and hand, the pelvic girdle, the leg and foot. The biggest bone in the body is the thigh bone or femur. In most adults it comprises 25% of our total height.

Bones tend to be classified in one of four groups: long, short, flat, or irregular. All bones are formed to fulfill specific tasks and needs. An observation from the National Space Biomedical Research Institute gives us a sense of this well-crafted design: "The arrangement of individual bones is as precise, orderly and purposeful as the full skeletal system itself, and their distribution from top to bottom is extremely balanced. Most of the bones in our body are structured in a symmetrical fashion."[14] This matched design, each side of the body's bones mirroring the other, allow us to have balance and stability.

Healthy bone is made up of a hard, solid outer structure called compact bone and an inner part called cancellous bone. Compact bone looks a little like ivory—and when you see bones in a biology lab or in a physical anthropology exhibit, this is what you are seeing. The inner bone looks somewhat like a sponge, or a very fine honeycomb. Within this inner bone, a network of tiny pieces of bone is filled with both red marrow, found at the end of bones, and yellow marrow, which is mostly fat and is found in the middle part of the bone. The red marrow contains stem cells; these are used in a variety of medical therapies, including treatment for Parkinson's disease.

In general, bones do four things: rebuild themselves, produce blood cells, protect the brain and other organs, and help maintain a steady amount of calcium in the body. At every moment, even when we are sitting still and breathing quietly, there is a hum of activity inside our bones. Old cells are being disposed of, and new cells are being created. In 2005, scientists discovered that our bones have a kind of "glue" that connects the protein fibers within them. This substance helps the body absorb shock in a fall, and it helps the bones repair if a break does occur. One researcher called this glue "molecular shock absorbers."[15]

Because they are hard, we often think of our bones as static, when in fact they are characterized by ongoing metabolic transformation. Both phosphorus and calcium are stored within the bones, and the right amount of each of these minerals is essential to the healthy working of the organs of the body. The bones release calcium and phosphorus as the body needs them, when certain hormones trigger that response. As those of us who live with osteoporosis know, sometimes too much calcium is removed from the bones, and they weaken for lack of sufficient amounts of that mineral. Continually, in a daily process of dying and renewal, old bone is sloughed off and old bone cells excreted as new bone keeps on forming. This happens at a slower rate as we age, but nevertheless the process continues, day in and day out.

Our bones are also the only part of the body that survives over time. At burial, if the body is not embalmed, the soft tissues (organs, muscles, nerves, etc.) eventually decompose, leaving only the skeletal structure behind. As we know from archaeological finds, bones may endure for centuries. Our bones support us all the day long, and they endure after our death.

~~~~~

Gracious God, you have created every bone in my body and arranged those bones in a wondrous design. I give you thanks for the strength of these bones, for their ability to heal and for their variety. May I remember those whose bones are not well formed, and those whose bodies suffer from skeletal malformation. I bless you for my creation, preservation, and the blessing of this life. Amen.

Practices

1. Go to this website (*www.innerbody.com/image/skelfov. html*) for an image of the human skeleton. As you move the

cursor around it, clicking for more information as you wish, take the time to make an intentional connection between the image you are studying and your own skeleton. Pay attention to the variety of bones and their arrangement. Spend as long as you wish exploring the image of the bones of the body. Then offer a prayer of thanksgiving for your bones.

2. Place your hands on your ribcage. Breathe deeply and notice the movement of the ribs. Then move your hands to your collarbone, and as you breathe notice its movement as well. Allow yourself to be aware of the ways in which the ribs protect your inner organs, and the design of ribcage and collarbone that permits this movement with the breath. Try breathing gently and deeply into your back, sensing the expansion of the ribs as they connect to your spine. With each breath, taken as prayer, repeat "Encompass me" (inhalation), "dear Friend" (exhalation).

3. Your femur (thighbone) is the largest bone in your body. Place your hands gently on your thighs, palm down. As you move the hands gently from knee to hip, notice the length of this bone. Become aware of its sturdy strength. Call to mind all the work this bone does in standing, walking, sitting, running, kneeling. Quietly form a prayer of thanks for the femur.

4. Our bones are held together by ligaments and cartilage; these connections are known as joints. The joints all do a lot of work, whether they are our ankles, our knees, our wrists, or our shoulders. If one of your joints is prone to pain or fatigue, place your hand gently on that joint. Give thanks for the continual work that it does. If you wish, bless the joint for its labor: "Gracious God, bless this joint as your own handiwork. Help me to be mindful of the nutrition and exercise that it needs to do what it is created to do. Amen."

5. In Psalm 35:10 the speaker says, "My very bones will say, 'LORD, who is like you?'" In Hebrew the word for "bone" (*estem*) also means "substance" or "self." In your journal, write down this verse from Psalm 35. Then trace your non-dominant hand. Sketch the bones within the hand (take the time to feel the bones to give yourself an idea of their arrangement.) Then rest your non-dominant hand in your dominant one, visualizing the bones, and pray, "My very bones will say, 'LORD, who is like you?'" Imagine your very bones resounding with wonder and praise. What images, sensations, memories, and associations does this bring? Close with a simple prayer of thanksgiving.

11

The Blood

Coursing throughout our entire body, bringing nutrients and oxygen to every tissue and every cell, our blood is essential to human life. There is no substitute for human blood, and no synthetic or manufactured substance that can do its work. Only a transfusion of blood will accomplish the task of replenishing blood loss.

On this essential physiological level, clearly blood and life are intimately connected. Without blood, we cannot live. Donating blood allows those who have lost too much of their own blood to survive. The blood offered literally becomes one with the blood of the person receiving the transfusion, and life is restored. Both the Hebrew scriptures and the Greek New Testament point us toward the intimate connection between life and blood. In the depiction of the last supper in the gospel of Matthew, Jesus says of the wine being shared, "Drink from it, all of you; for this is my blood of the covenant, which is poured out for many for the forgiveness of sin" (Matt. 26:27). The wine represents blood, which in turn represents life; these associations are deep and ancient.

As you probably know, our blood is mainly made up of plasma, red blood cells, white blood cells, and platelets. Just over half of the blood is plasma, which, when separated from the other cells, looks like yellowish water. Plasma also contains proteins and salts, and serves as the carrier for the red and white blood cells and the platelets. Our blood looks red to our eyes because of the red blood cells, whose color comes from the iron they contain.

Our bones, as you will recall, are the sites of the creation of new blood cells. In adults, the marrow in the vertebrae, hips, ribs, skull, and sternum are the primary sites of this process. A healthy adult has about ten pints of blood in the body, and that blood usually makes up about seven percent of our total body weight. If a person loses more than forty percent of total blood volume, survival is unlikely. The heart would not have a sufficient volume of blood to keep the body nourished, and the whole body would suffer from the consequences.

Our red blood cells distribute oxygen throughout the tissues of the body, and pick up the waste gas—carbon dioxide—so that it can be expelled through the lungs during exhalation. Hemoglobin, a protein in the red blood cells, contains iron; the hemoglobin is the carrier for both the oxygen and the carbon dioxide. As the hemoglobin in the red blood cells moves throughout the body, this inner respiration is continually happening. These hard-working red blood cells have a life span of about four months. We have more red blood cells than any other kind in the body.

The white blood cells are the workhorses of our immune systems. There are a variety of white blood cells with different functions—some target bacteria, some viruses, and some cancer cells. The body's ability to protect itself from infection is amazing. For example, if bacteria enter the body through a small cut, the white blood cells identify the intruder and engulf it. These cells are somewhat like sentries, continually watching for the presence of virus, bacteria, or other cells that are dead or malformed. The life span of white blood cells varies with the type of cell, but none last longer than a few months.

Platelets are essential to clotting or coagulation of the blood. They only survive nine days, so have to be created quickly within the marrow. If a cut or an injury occurs, the platelets and other clotting factors in the blood are responsible for stopping the flow of blood and allowing for a scab to form—a process we easily take for granted. The platelets, clotting factors, and fibrin create the scab, which keeps germs out and protects the injured skin as healing takes place and new skin is formed. Of course, if a cut or an injury is too big for a clot to form, stitches or surgery may be needed.

In addition to transporting oxygen, disposing of carbon dioxide, fighting infection, and creating clotting as needed, the blood also:

- removes other waste products like urea from the body,
- transports hormones,
- regulates the acidity of the body (pH), and
- regulates our body temperature by sending more blood to the surface when it is hot, and less blood when we are chilled.

Though the rate of speed varies with the size of the blood vessel, the blood makes a complete circuit of the body in about a minute. In the time it has taken you to read this far in this chapter, therefore, unless you are very fast, your blood has made the full circuit from your heart to your hands and feet, and back again. Though you may observe yourself to be quietly reading (and from one perspective, you are), within your body the blood is moving, circulating, and flowing from heart to organs to muscle to capillaries and back again. Sometimes it is moving as fast as ten miles per hour!

As this movement continues, so does the process of inner respiration. We have come full circle, back to the heart and the lungs, whose functions allow the blood to transport oxygen, nutrients, hormones, sugar, and other substances to every cell in the body.

God of Life and Love, I give you thanks for the blood that circulates throughout my body. I give thanks for red blood cells, white blood cells, plasma, and platelets. You have created blood to cleanse, nourish, repair, and protect the body. May I remember those who need blood this day, and may I never forget those who generously give of their life blood that others might live. Amen.

Practices

1. Sitting quietly, remember the last time that you suffered a small cut that did not require stitches. Perhaps you nicked a finger while chopping vegetables or were cut by a small shard of glass while gardening. Remember the rapidity with which the bleeding stopped. Allow your imagination to create an image of the platelets and clotting factors working at the site of injury to stop the flow of blood. Give thanks for your blood's health and for the marvel of these cells.

2. Sitting or lying quietly, begin by breathing deeply and gently. Once your breath has found its own rhythm, place two fingers of one hand on the right or left side of your neck, so that you can feel your pulse through the artery. As you feel the blood pump through the artery, remember that within a minute it will be returning to the heart. Gently pay attention to the rhythmic, steady coursing of the blood and give thanks for its work throughout your organs, brain, muscles, and cells. Allow yourself to rest in the awareness of the blood's movement and the microscopic transformations occurring even as you pray. Remember that each cell of your blood has its own distinctive gifts and responsibilities, and give thanks.

3. One website describes the white blood cells as "mobile warriors in the battle against infection and invasion."[16] Whenever we catch a cold or the flu, our white blood cells are fighting that virus. Rest, nutrition and exercise

appropriate to your physical state all benefit this immune function. As you reflect on the work of the white blood cells and their role in your health, what adjustments might you want to make with regard to getting adequate sleep, eating according to a healthier pattern, or choosing to exercise in a way that fits your age and interests? (For example, some might choose tennis while others will prefer yoga; some might prefer walking in the outdoors while others will be more inclined to work out in a gym.) Begin to recognize that your practices with regard to physical well-being have an essential spiritual aspect. *Grateful* care of your body is a very different way of engaging your own physicality. Try to engage nutrition, rest, and exercise as a way of giving thanks and befriending your blood and organs.

Finally, in your journal, list three ways in which you hope to befriend your blood and your body. This could include regular exercise, eating vegetables that contain iron (such as spinach, lima beans or Swiss chard), or refraining from processed foods.

PART 3

Showing Forth Gratitude

This last section of the book is an invitation for you to show forth gratitude for your body and care for the bodies of others. Our bodies quite literally connect us with one another—through touch, through breast feeding, through love making. Our bodies, these God-given primary habitats, show forth divine handiwork. They are also finite; we know our days are numbered because the body may succumb to any number of maladies or accidents. Even if we live to be one hundred years old, over time the body simply wears out and shuts down.

Becoming contemplatively aware of our bodies leads us more deeply into gratefulness. The gratefulness will organically flow into care and compassion for the bodies of others. As Brother David Steindl-Rast has observed, when we become aware of this world (and, by extension, our bodies) as a blessing, given by God—this God who works creatively and persistently with matter—we find ourselves wanting to bless and gift others.[17] In English the words "blessing" and "blood" are closely related; to "bless" originally referred to sprinkling blood upon a pagan altar. Just as our blood circulates throughout our bodies, restoring, replenishing, and healing, so our spirits are intended to circulate gratitude through action. We are created to become beings that are related to others and to the world we have been given. As we grow in our capacity to remember that we have been created in the image and likeness of this God who dwells in matter and in bodies, holding it all together, our hearts and minds awaken to a larger sense of purpose. We join with the early church in first-century Colossae, singing, "Christ is the image of the invisible God, the first born of all creation; for in him all things in heaven and on earth were created, things visible and invisible, whether thrones or dominions or rulers or powers—all things have been created through him and for him. He himself is before all things and in him all things hold together" (Col. 1:15-17).

As we behold and befriend our bodies, our eyes begin to catch glimpses of the presence of Christ in and through everything. Our false sense of entitlement and our narcissistic isolation erode gently under the gaze of love. We find ourselves repenting of our tendency to overlook what we do not want to see and to choose blindness instead. The indwelling presence of Christ, in whom all things hold together, challenges our assumptions and confronts us with our own greed and self-centeredness.

This is not a particularly comfortable moment in the spiritual journey, of course. We discover what the desert elders knew in the fourth and fifth centuries: the journey is a struggle. We try to persevere with good humor in faith, hope, and love. At our best, we encourage one another to allow the equipoise of spiritual balance to find us, rather than zealously charging around and challenging others to see the truth as we see it.

Gratefulness moves us beyond the "I've got it!" mentality that pervades some versions of spirituality. By definition, growing in gratitude leads us into deepening awareness of interconnection and interdependence. When my right hand was in a cast and I was unable to do a number of daily tasks, my husband Doug stepped in to do more of the grocery shopping, the cooking, the cleaning, the washing. Friends and family came to our aid. My son checked in regularly to see how I was progressing. My surgeon and her staff offered so much encouragement. The physical therapist kept me laughing as we tried to move fingers that seemed stuck at the time. My massage therapist gently moved my hand, arm and wrist, and said one day, "There is so much life in this limb!" I had to marvel at the web of support that surrounded me. All of those relationships sprang into a specific kind of embodied action, and I found it to be distinctly humbling to be the recipient of that kind of attention and care.

I also remembered the reality for which we are created, the truth in which we dwell without being fully aware. In the words of Archbishop Desmond Tutu,

> We say a person is a person through other persons. . . . We learn how to think, how to walk, how to speak, how to behave—indeed, how to be human—from other human beings. We need other human beings in order to be human. We are made for togetherness, we are made for family, for fellowship, to exist in a tender network of interdependence.[18]

I use the word "remember" intentionally, for like many of us I fall into a radical kind of forgetting. I forget that our very being, our created, redeemed, and sanctified reality is inherently grounded in the God who is Trinity. I fall asleep to the stunning revelation that God in Christ, through the power of the Holy Spirit, *is* community, a community so profoundly loving that sacred Oneness is known in that love.

So as I continue to go to the hand surgeon's office and have x-rays, I am much aware of every other patient in the waiting room. I watch the interactions between the patients, the staff, and the nurses, and see how beautiful the medicine of encouragement and kindness is. I behold my doctor's joy in a patient's healing, and her care when a break is not mending as it should. I watch an ongoing exchange of gratefulness—patients for the doctor and nurses, nurses for the doctor, and the doctor for staff, nurses, and patients. Something palpable indwells that space that is rooted and grounded in love, as well as in skill, training, and diagnostic precision. Gratefulness leads us to receive the life we have been given. Gratefulness allows us to live in the present, to slow down, to stop and notice who might need our help. We remember to circulate the gift of life, blessing the bodies of others and the body of our planet in myriad ways.

The chapters that follow offer some possibilities for embodying gratefulness, for making it as natural as breathing, as steady as the pulse of blood in your arteries. Gratefulness allows life to circulate—just like blood—nourishing the larger body of humanity. The word "thanksgiving" is built on the two components, "thanks" and "giving." Giving is an organic response to receiving the gift of life and the gift of our bodies. An inherent circulatory capacity awakens within us as we grow in gratitude. Giving reveals itself as an innate, gracious dimension of human life.

This last section of the book is not an invitation for you to participate in every single suggestion. That would be both impossible and maddening. Rather, I am offering a variety of possibilities for you to circulate the gift of life, with intentional desire to honor the bodies of the whole human family. As you read these final chapters, therefore, be attentive to what quickens your spirit and what kindles your imagination. This is an invitation to remember that you, as a member of the body of humanity, have a hidden and transformative purpose, and that your willingness to participate in God's love for all that has been created may take surprisingly mundane and incarnate forms. Perhaps you will donate blood. Perhaps you will register with a program for organ donation. Maybe you will awaken to care for the water, air, and dirt of the world in which we live. Whatever your response, remember that each action circulates the gift, each compassionate step forward quickens the body of this world, held together by Christ himself.

12

Circulating Life
with Clean Water

We begin our lives within the enclosed amniotic sea of our mother's womb. When we are very young, we are "watery" beings; a baby's body is almost eighty percent water. As we age, that begins to diminish, though water is clearly necessary for human life. Over half the adult human body, approximately sixty percent, is water.

We need clean water to survive. Our bodies need water for blood and for our organs. Water is the means by which our bodies are internally cleansed and restored; without it, the body's temperature cannot be regulated. Because it is a solvent, water helps dissolve what needs to be dissolved and then excretes those elements out of the body through urination. Water is imperative for a healthy body.

As we turn to reflecting on the body of the planet, we are told that about seventy percent of the earth's surface is water. The oceans hold most of it, while rivers, streams, lakes, glaciers, and water vapor make up the remaining five percent. An article from the United States Geological Survey observes, "Water on, in and above the Earth is never sitting still, and thanks to the water cycle, our planet's water supply is constantly moving from one place to another and from one form to another. Things would get pretty stale without the water cycle!"[19]

Given these facts, we might assume that clean water is readily available for the health and well-being of creatures and humans throughout the world. However, that is not the case. According to Waterlines, a non-profit organization dedicated to making clean water available throughout the world, approximately a billion people are without it. So many diseases are linked to the lack of fresh, unpolluted water; so many bodies suffer from lack of adequate hydration. Furthermore, in many parts of the world it is women who are given the task of trekking to wells for water, often over long distances. Waterlines reports that in sub-Saharan Africa, on the average, a woman walks six kilometers a day in order to find it—and the water she does find is often cloudy and unclean. Yet families, children, and the elderly depend on the labor of these women to bring water home. Their lives quite literally depend on it.

As you sit and read this book, in all probability safe drinking water is something you take for granted. You turn on a faucet and there is water; you know it is drinkable, and that your local government tests it from time to time for contaminants. Your city, county, and state governments help provide the infrastructure necessary for water to be delivered to your home, office, or school. When you want to make coffee or tea, or boil pasta, or prepare a soup, you don't have to think twice about whether the water is usable. Even if you have personal standards that lead you not to use water straight out of the tap, you probably use a water filter to distill and clean it. In short, if you are reading this book, in all probability you are not walking for six kilometers to get water so that your body may be hydrated.

⌒

O God you have wonderfully created and yet more wonderfully restored humanity in your Son Jesus Christ. You have created our bodies in the waters of our mothers' wombs, and through the great waters you brought the Israelites out of Egypt into the promised land. As we partake of the water you have provided, may we be ever mindful of those who do not

*have clean water. May we offer our memory, reason, and skill
as instruments of grace that we may find ways to distribute
the resource of water throughout the world, for the blessing of
the bodies of those whom you have made. Amen.*

Practices

1. Begin to notice your own thirst. It is easy to mistake being
thirsty for being hungry, so try drinking water instead
of eating the next time you think you are hungry—you
may be surprised. Ask yourself: "How do I know that I
am thirsty? How is that registered in my body?" This may
seem like a strange question, but it is worth pondering.
What tells you that you need a drink of water? How do you
become aware of thirst? When you register thirst, do you
drink water or something else?

   Now imagine being thirsty and not being able to readily acquire water. Imagine the thirst beginning to increase,
and not having the means to slake it. As you imagine this,
call to awareness all those who thirst but have no water,
or who only have dirty, stale water to drink. Call to mind
those whose bodies languish for lack of adequate clean
water. Quietly sit with this awareness, praying, "Lord,
have mercy." Stay with this prayer as long as you wish, and
return to it as you are led. Notice how your own attention
and compassion for those without water begins to change.
Be alert to any desire to offer concrete help, to be active
in bringing clean water to those whose bodies thirst for it.

2. Create a prayer of thanksgiving for clean water and for
being able to drink it without fretting about contaminants.
Give thanks for those who tend your local water supply,
and for the regulations that ensure its safety, including
those who tend local waterlines and who restore broken
water mains. If your community participates in water con-
servation programs, familiarize yourself with ways in which
you can conserve water. For example, in San Antonio we

have been enduring a drought of epic proportions. It has made us all much more "water-wise," and we are increasingly aware of ways to economize on our use of water for bathing, cooking, and gardening, as well as to guard the health of rivers, streams, and reservoirs.)

3. Throughout the world, around one billion people do not have access to clean water. Their bodies are weakened because of this, making them more prone to illness and to malnutrition. Clean water is essential for the flourishing of the body. Consider contributing to organizations that support the development of clean water systems throughout those areas whose water supplies are compromised. An organization called Waterlines (*www.waterlines.org*) offers a variety of ways for you to be active and involved in the development of water supplies throughout the world.

13

Circulating Life through Food

E very body needs water, food, and air as fuel to keep going. Optimally, that food will be full of nutrients and free of contaminants such as toxins or additives. For our organs to do the work they have been given to do, they need both adequate hydration and nutrition. As we have seen, our organs labor constantly. Our various metabolic processes transpire without much attention on our part. Food gets digested. Toxins are eliminated. Cells wear out, and new cells are created. Nerves signal the brain when we are hot or cold, tired or alert, hungry or thirsty.

The body needs food in order to function well. Without it the organs cannot do their work efficiently and thoroughly. Tending to the nutritional needs of your own body is a way of responding to the gift of life. If you find that you've been instructed to follow a particular dietary plan, and are also encountering a lot of inner resistance, remember that your faithfulness to eating responsibly is a way to celebrate life. Remember that your organs, muscles, brain, skin, and bones need food that will support their work, not food that just fills your stomach.

In a way, eating with this kind of mindfulness is a way of befriending the body you have been given. Over time, care in meal planning and preparation, and joy in food on the table, become practices that allow for friendly regard for those organs that are working so hard. Eating becomes less an unconscious matter of "fueling up," and more a manner of communion—not only with those with whom you dine and those who have grown the food, but with your own physicality. This won't happen overnight. Just like any shift in perception and attention, it will take time and patience.

You might start with tracking the number of times that you eat out during a week. Write down what you eat. Then take the time to do some online research with regard to the food value in what you are eating. Watch for elevated levels of sugar, salt, fat, and additives. Having spent some time reflecting on the work your organs do, imagine, for example, the burden imposed upon them by excess sodium. Imagine the effect on your blood, on your kidneys, and on your digestive tract. Remember the body's need to keep sodium and potassium in balance, and recognize that high amounts of sodium will cause the body to labor in an effort to clear the excess from blood and organs.

Notice that your intention in this practice is one of gratefulness, not guilt. As you reflect on how you eat and what you eat, seek to be kindly aware of this gift of physicality. Allow yourself to befriend the body that you have been given. As a spiritual director who sometimes works with people who have suffered from illness, I often hear the phrase, "I feel like my body betrayed me." On the one hand, this is an understandable response, and one that needs to be held gently and explored. On the other, we also betray our bodies in so many ways, including the regular ingestion of foods that do not foster health or of quantities of food that are disproportionate to the needs of the body.

Our need to eat and drink also reminds us that we are interconnected. The food we eat is almost always grown or raised by someone else, either locally or half a world away. Someone has transported that food to a grocery store or to a farmers' market. Someone has sold it to us. All of those people—growers, harvesters, truckers, and vendors—have literally had a hand in the movement of food from its place of origin to our mouths and bodies. As author Wendell Berry has observed, "This pleasure is perhaps the profoundest enactment of our connection with the world. In this pleasure we experience and celebrate our dependence and our gratitude, for we are living from mystery, from creatures we did not make and powers we cannot comprehend."[20]

As you begin to be mindful of how your body is fueled and fed, allow yourself also to be mindful of the needs of others. You may want to visit a local food bank or donate to an organization that fights world hunger, such as Bread for the World or Oxfam. You may become interested in the patterns of drought and crop failure around the planet, and find yourself led to support organizations that advocate for changes in government policies. As you become more deeply grateful for your own body, that gratefulness may propel you to join efforts to circulate the gift of food.

⸺⸻

Gracious Lover of souls and bodies, grant me the desire to tend this body with gentle care, the will to choose well and the wisdom to honor your gift. Help me to remember those whose bodies lack nutritional food, both in my community and throughout the world. Guide me to be a companion to those in need. Amen.

Practices

1. Make a list of your favorite foods. Start this list now, and add to it over time. Don't censure the list—if you love chicken fried steak, put it down! As you write down these favorites, note the variety, whether it means variety of ethnic cuisines, kinds of food (fruits, breads, vegetables, fish), or styles of preparation (apples, applesauce, apple

fritters, apple dumplings, baked apples). Pay attention to the memories and associations that you have with these foods. Perhaps peaches remind you of summers as a child, or olives take you back to a trip to the Mediterranean. Allow yourself to spend some time with the connections that come to mind. Then create a prayer of thanksgiving for these foods, for your acquaintance with them, for your enjoyment of them, and for the ways in which they have been sacred connections to life and friends, memory and feasting.

2. After becoming aware of this variety of foods and the delight that they bring, focus on the fact that many people around the world do not have the happy choice of various foods. Indeed, many people have little food to eat, even in the United States. In 2010, 14.5 percent of American households (17.2 million households) were what is known as "food insecure"—approximately one in seven households lacked adequate food. Worldwide, it is estimated that 925 million people suffer from hunger.[21] Those who live in refugee camps where some food stuffs are provided by international relief agencies often eat the same food day after day, simply to stay alive. Those who live in regions of famine or disaster do not have access to a variety of food, while people living within miles of your home may not have enough money to purchase a healthy variety of food. For example, a young girl told the personnel at the San Antonio Food Bank that she was delighted with that week's delivery of food for her family because she had never tasted raspberries before, and that week's donations included pints of raspberries from a local grocer.

3. As a way to embody gratefulness for the foods that you enjoy and that fuel your body, consider doing one of the following:

   • Support a local food bank with monetary donations or by volunteering.

- Donate to world relief agencies such as Bread for the World.

- Contact a local school district with the intention of supporting nutritional options for students.

- Support and encourage your local farmers markets, especially those with extension programs to supply fresh food to poorer families.

4. Author Alice Peck has observed, "Every bite we chew merits our attention. It's a quick prayer. A moment for meditation. An opportunity to pause and recognize our place in the food chain, to appreciate our great fortune at having food on our plates, to check in with ourselves and to savor our connection to the universe. It's remarkable that a mere omelet, a Brussels sprout, or a piece of candy corn holds so much power. Every morsel we consume gives us another opportunity to see the Sacred."[22] At your next meal, allow yourself a moment for meditation as you dine. Savor what you are eating, and notice the beauty of the food. Give thanks for those whose labor has brought that food to your plate. Resolve to aid those who hunger for food throughout the world.

14

Circulating the Gift through the Donation of Blood

B lood is essential for life. There is no substitute for it, and no synthetic or manufactured substance will do. When blood is needed during surgery or after an accident or a disaster, blood banks provide the needed supplies. The American Red Cross states that at every moment someone needs blood—the need is constant. One pint of blood can save three lives. If your health permits, giving blood quite literally circulates the gift of life.

My sister Susie, who provided so much of the inspiration for this book, gives blood as often as is medically permitted, and has donated many pints over the years. As a nurse, she constantly witnesses occasions when blood is a matter of life and death in the hospital. My church community, St. Mark's Episcopal Church in San Antonio, regularly holds blood drives. I am often struck by the presence of the blood donation RV in our parking lot on those Sundays, and by the direct connection made by parishioners who have just received communion, and then donate blood. The embodied life of God and the gifted nature of that life are made quite visible on those occasions.

If you are a potential donor, and have questions about the process, you can find clear answers at the Red Cross website, and if you cannot donate blood, you can encourage those who participate in blood drives through prayer.

Gracious God, you have appointed the organs and systems of our bodies, and have brought forth our circulatory systems so that life-sustaining blood may nourish our cells. May we be led to donate our blood in your Name, that those who receive may receive life. Amen.

Practices

1. Before you donate blood, be sure to have a light meal and to drink water or juice. As you partake of this food and drink, remember that you are nourishing your own body that it may provide blood for others. Give thanks for your body's ability to regenerate blood cells, and for the technicians who will draw the blood and tend you during the donation process.

2. While your blood is being drawn, offer a silent prayer of blessing for those who will receive it: "Bless those who will receive the blessing of this blood with which You have blessed me."

3. Later in the day, having returned to your home, be sure to follow the instructions given to you by the blood bank personnel and to allow your own body to rest. As you rest, give thanks for your body, for the gift of your own blood, for your body's ability to adapt to the somewhat diminished blood volume. Give thanks for those who have tended you during this process. Then quietly place two fingers on the pulse point on either side of your neck (where the carotid artery is just below the surface), and silently become aware of the circulation of your own blood, now given for the lives of others.

15

Circulating Life
through Organ Donation

Late last spring, a family member of ours died in his mid-twenties. Before his death, Sean had become aware of the work of the Texas Organ Sharing Alliance, so when he was renewing his driver's license, it seemed right to sign up with the Texas Organ Sharing Association so that in the event of his death, his organs would be donated to others. T.O.S.A. states that when someone registers to be an organ donor, as many as eight other lives may be saved. In Sean's case, four patients awaiting transplant received the gift of his organs and were all allowed to begin life anew.

At the time of his death, his parents and his brother were called upon to make a decision about whether or not to honor Sean's desire to donate his organs. They all knew he had signed up with the organ registry, and they wanted to honor his wishes. The personnel from T.O.S.A. answered many questions and also went through an extensive questionnaire with Sean's family. Once it was determined that brain death had transpired, a process that took about two days, Sean's body was taken to the operating room, and the procedure to remove his organs for transplant began.

One of the last acts that took place in Sean's room in the ICU before his body went to surgery was the celebration of

Holy Communion. We stood around his bed, prayed for him and for those who would receive his organs, and shared the bread and the wine. We prayed the Lord's Prayer together. We blessed Sean and gave thanks for his life. At this moment I could not help but see Sean's body as an altar, a place of gathering for communion.

From the operating room, his organs were sent forth. Sean's parents and brother have received letters from the organ recipients, letters full of gratefulness for Sean's generosity and for the family's fidelity to that generosity. The letters reassure the family of the gift of Sean's life. Each letter is a witness to a life extended through Sean's intention to share his body. Sean's care for others led me and my husband to register with the Texas Organ Sharing Alliance as well, in addition to indicating on our driver's licenses that we are willing to be organ donors.

The United States Department of Health and Human Services website notes that over 100,000 people are waiting for an organ transplant. Every eleven minutes, a new potential recipient is added to the organ donation registry; in most cases, these are people who are in end-stage of organ failure. Sometimes a person is in need of corneas or skin or bone. In addition, eighteen people on waiting lists for organ transplant die per day because the demand is so much greater than the resources, while an average of seventy-five people receive an organ or tissue transplant daily. As an article on the department's website remarks, "One thing to remember is that every number in the statistic you view is a person, a person who either needs your help and is waiting for a life-saving transplant or a person who has left a lasting legacy through organ and tissue donation. Either way, each number represents a life, a mom, a dad, a brother, a sister or a child, someone who is important to someone else, maybe even you." And in case you are wondering whether organ transplantation is successful, statistics from May 2009 report the following percentages of people who were living five years after their transplant:

- Kidney 69.3%
- Heart 74.9%
- Liver 73.8%
- Lung 54.4%[23]

With each year that goes by, moreover, further research allows the success rate of organ transplant to increase. It is also worth remembering that transplant of bone, bone marrow, skin, and corneas are all needed in situations of severe injury, combat wounds, and accidents.

While most of us may think of organ donation as something that would happen after our deaths, living donors may also donate a kidney or a part of the pancreas, lung, liver, or intestine. Becoming a living donor should be done only after due consideration with physicians and family members, especially the latter, because this generous decision can be a difficult topic to discuss with our families and decide upon for ourselves. Furthermore, it is a major surgical procedure. Because our bodies can compensate for a missing kidney or a piece of the lung, liver, pancreas, or intestine, a living donor does undertake some risk and faces a long period of recuperation after the surgery.

Catholicism, Protestantism, Islam, and most branches of Judaism allow for organ donation. If you have questions about the teaching of your own faith tradition with regard to organ donation, you can visit *organdonor.gov/about/religious views.html*, which lists the views of many different branches of faith traditions. The 70th General Convention of the Episcopal Church recommended and urged "all members of this Church to consider seriously the opportunity to donate organs after death that others may live, and that such decision be clearly stated to family, friends, church and attorney." (Resolution 1991-AO97)[24]

⌒

Gracious and life giving God, we know from the scriptural story that you are a God who brings life out of death. As I

*consider becoming an organ donor, guide me by your Holy
Spirit to remember those whose lives will be extended by the gift
of organs. May I offer this body for the life of others. Amen.*

Practices

1. As you consider the possibility of becoming an organ
   donor, what feelings, memories, and associations come
   to your awareness? Do you notice any resistance? Gently
   observe your own thoughts and feelings, and notice how
   this possibility registers in your own body. Be mindful that
   this would be a choice freely offered in love, and allow
   yourself the freedom to choose without guilt or coercion.

2. If you decide that you would like to become an organ
   donor, you may go to the website of the United States
   Department of Health and Human Services for a link to
   your state's donor registration program: *organdonor.gov/
   becomingdonor/index.html.* Before registering, quietly give
   thanks for your organs and tissue. After registering, if you
   wish, pray, "Upon my death, may these organs go forth to
   do the work they have been given to do."

3. I know three adults whose lives have been extended by a
   living donor who has offered a kidney, and in each case,
   a family member proved to be a match. I also know a
   woman who received a portion of an adult liver from
   a donor in another state when hers succumbed to disease; in this case the match was made without familial
   connection. In each of these cases, the recipient has
   journeyed deeply into spiritual and physical hospitality
   and gratefulness. The liver recipient said, "I feel as if
   my whole body is welcoming a stranger who has brought
   the gift of life." Those who receive organ transplant
   are pioneers in the journey of gratefulness. If you have
   received an organ, or are preparing to do so, bless your
   donor in your prayers, and give thanks for the life you
   have received.

Conclusion

Your Works Are Wonderful, and I Know It Well

O ur bodies are gifts, and these gifts are outward and visible signs of God's own life—creating, redeeming, and sanctifying—right here, right now. Our bodies reveal both intricate care in design and mystery in their various processes of transformation. As we befriend our bodies, we learn to honor and to tend them. As we begin to know a little about all that transpires within our organs without our conscious participation, we begin to move toward the wisdom of Dag Hammarskjold: "For all that has been—thanks. For all that will be—yes." The body is itself a sacrament, an outward and visible sign of God's presence in all places and at all times. We remember that that presence is always active, compassionate, bringing life out of death. As an Eastern Orthodox saying reminds us, "There is no place where God is not," and we should not be surprised that it includes the physical reality of our own breathing, digesting, and eliminating selves.

Over twenty-five years ago, when I first began to practice yoga and learn a bit about breathing, muscles, and the spine, I began to realize that for many of us today the spiritual path begins with befriending one's own body. If we learn basic anatomy and take the time to know the art and poetry of the body's design, we will find ourselves echoing the psalms and making their words our own: "Your works are wonderful, and I know it well" (Ps.139:13). We might find ourselves humbled before the wondrous arrangement of the organs themselves. We might be led to quiet pondering of the fact of the circulation of our blood, and be stunned by all that we have taken for granted. Sitting in a doctor's examination room, hearing the words, "It is benign," we might be swept up by a tide of gratefulness that leads to care in honoring a life restored. Or it may be that we hear, "This is a malignancy," and begin to honor the body's diligent work in living with cancer treatment.

When we come home to our bodies, we come home to our souls. We discover that this "humus," this matter that makes up our physicality, is the very stuff that is honored in the conception, birth, life, and death of Jesus. We find that the God who makes dirt is a God who loves bodies, all bodies. We discover that our physical selves are indeed *capax dei*, with the capacity for being indwelt by the living God, because that is how our bodies are constituted. They would not exist were it not for the gracious work and creative joy of the living God who brings them into being. These bodies are abodes for God. As Jesus remarks in the gospel of John, "Those who love me will keep my word, and my Father will love them, and we will come to them, and make our home with them" (John 14:23).

Yes, your physical being, transitory as it is, knows God's presence. Your very cells are created by love, with love, and in love. This is scandalous, of course. When we realize that God's infinite mercy and love extends to every particle of the universe (otherwise how would it exist?) and that our bodies are included in that enveloping mercy and love, we may be disconcerted. It is always easier to hold God at arm's length. As various saints and mystics over the centuries have observed, it is often the intimacy of God's presence that we can't abide.

If this living God in Christ is closer to me than my cells, can I bear that revelation? If this body is marvelously made, can I embrace that awareness?

Our bodies are of infinite worth in God's sight because they are God's own creation. Every single body is a creative expression of God's own life and care. That may not be what you have been taught, nor the perspective that you hold. However, this is the perspective of the God who chooses to indwell a human body, whose own Light and Life bring everything into being. In the prologue of the gospel of John we are reminded, "All things came into being through him, and without him not one thing came into being" (John 1:3). All things, all matter, and all bodies have come into being through Christ. Your body came into being through the living Word who is the Christ, the living God and the God of the living. Every sub-atomic particle, every atom, every molecule, every cell came into being through God's own life and work. Allowing ourselves to receive this awareness turns everything on its head. Our bodies are temples. Our bodies are not only our primary habitat; they are God's habitat.

Throughout this book, you and I together have been discovering what has been with us all along, hidden yet fully present. Each of the organs that we have noticed and given thanks for was created in our mother's wombs, and each bone of our skeleton first formed when we were still in that watery region. Our blood, our nerves, our lymphatic system—all that is the body—came into being without our aid. All of those organs and systems speak volumes of the intimate presence of God's own tender, creative presence. Our own physicality, so deprecated and distorted by advertising and mass media, turns out to be truly a temple. These bodies are not unlike medieval abbeys, full of architectural harmony, capacious spaces, and wondrous light, light that indwells all that exists. The molecular biologists tell us that most of an atom is space. Most of the space of our essential building blocks of molecules and cells is open, full of energy, mysteriously arranged to be alive. The body that is you, as you read these words, is an expression of divine vitality, vibrating with the love that speaks it into being. Your body, like all bodies, is a temple of the Holy Spirit and a dwelling place for the living Trinity of love.

Sometimes we see this presence in those we hold dear before we can behold it in ourselves. When my sons were young, I read them Madeleine L'Engle's series of novels that make up the Time Quintet. The author invites the reader on journeys both far and wide, journeys through the depths of time and far galaxies, and through the infinite spaces within the human cell. In the second book in the series, *A Wind in the Door*, the reader is introduced to a mitochondria, which is the energy unit of the cell. Named Sporos, this mitochondria is charged to be who he is and deepen in his own work and life. The life of a young man depends on Sporos' willingness to accept his own creation and identity, to stop whirling and spinning, to become his embodied self, and to participate in the vast whole that is the cosmos. I remember reading this to Bryan and Jason, and reflecting on their own young male bodies, growing and changing. I remember going to sleep giving thanks for their healthy bodies and for those startling moments when I could see the changes happening before my eyes. Within them, their own mitochondria were hard at work, busy in the work of cell division and differentia-tion, as each young boy began to grow toward puberty and then manhood.

We are all, each one of us, like Sporos the mitochondria. We have a choice so basic that it is easy to overlook or ignore. The living God who indwells our organs and blood, our mus-cles and bones, waits for us to stop our spinning and whirling. God patiently hopes that we will pause. God desires that we will be still. This gracious Creator wonders if we will direct our attention to the indwelling presence that crafts every cell of our bodies, every organ, every bone. Will we, like Sporos, come to know the startling reality revealed in the abode of the body? And then will we allow ourselves to see that same reality in every single body, every bit of matter, every context and circumstance in which we live?

At the beginning of this book I quoted theologian Sallie McFague: "The most prevalent spiritual disease of our time is not wanting to be here, not wanting to be in a physical body." As we start to notice the physical body that is our first home and our primary habitat, we are challenged by the sheer intimacy of divine presence. No wonder our Christian life proclaims resurrection of the body! This physicality is a wonder. This body is a marvelous work.

May you begin to listen to your body. May you honor this body that is God's own wonderful work. And may you regard the bodies of others as God does—worthy of creation, beautiful in arrangement, home to the One in whom we live and move and have our being.

For Further Reading

Gratefulness

Au, Wilkie and Noreen Cannon Au. *Grateful Heart: The Living Christian Message*. Mahwah, NJ: Paulist Press, 2011.

Chittister, Joan and Rowan Williams. *Uncommon Gratitude: Alleluia for All That Is*. Collegeville, MN: Liturgical Press, 2010.

Leddy, Mary Jo. *Radical Gratitude*. Maryknoll, NY: Orbis Books, 2002.

Steindel-Rast, David. Gratefulness, *The Heart of Prayer: An Approach to Life in Fullness*. Mahwah, NJ: Paulist Press, 1984.

Anatomy of the Body

Clayman, Charles, ed. *The Human Body: An Illustrated Guide to Its Structure, Function, and Disorders*. New York, NY: DK Publishers, 1995.

National Geographic Society and Sherwin B. Nuland. *Incredible Voyage: Exploring the Human Body*. Washington, DC: National Geographic Society, 1998.

Parker, Steve. *The Human Body Book*. New York, NY: DK Publishers, 2007.

Praying with the Body

DeLeon, Roy. *Praying with the Body: Bringing the Psalms to Life*. Brewster, MA: Paraclete Press, 2009.

Earle, Mary C. *Beginning Again: Benedictine Wisdom for Living with Illness*. Harrisburg, PA: Morehouse, 2004.

————. *Broken Body, Healing Spirit: Lectio Divina and Living with Illness.* Harrisburg, PA: Morehouse, 2003.

————. *Days of Grace: Meditations and Practices for Living with Illness.* Harrisburg, PA: Morehouse, 2009.

Newell, John Philip. *Echo of the Soul: The Sacredness of the Human Body.* Harrisburg, PA: Morehouse, 2002.

Pagitt, Doug and Kathryn Prill. *BodyPrayer: The Posture of Intimacy with God.* Colorado Springs, CO: WaterBrook Press, 2005.

Roth, Nancy. *Spiritual Exercises: Joining Body and Spirit in Prayer.* New York: Seabury Books, 2005.

Wuellner, Flora Slosson. *Prayers and Our Bodies.* Nashville, TN: Upper Room, 2005.

Helpful Websites

American Lung Association
www.lungusa.org

American Red Cross, Blood Donation
www.redcrossblood.org

How Stuff Works: Human Biology
science.howstuffworks.com/environmental/life/human-biology

Kids' Health: How the Body Works
kidshealth.org/kid/htbw/

The Mayo Clinic
www.mayoclinic.com/health

National Digestive Diseases Information Clearing House
digestive.niddk.nih.gov/ddiseases/pub/yrdd

National Geographic Health and Human Body
science.nationalgeographic.com/science/health-and-human-body/
human-body/

National Institutes of Health
health.nih.gov/

National Kidney Foundation
www.kidney.org

Waterlines
www.waterlines.org

Notes

1. Joan Borysenko, *Minding the Body, Mending the Mind* (New York: Bantam, 1987). The phrase "New Age fundamentalism" comes from a workshop that Joan Borysenko offered at Kanuga Conference Center during the Spiritual Formation Conference of April 2002.

2. For more on this topic see Mary C. Earle, *Broken Body, Healing Spirit: Lectio Divina and Living with Illness* (Harrisburg, PA: Morehouse, 2003).

3. See Frederic and Mary Ann Brussat, eds., *Spiritual Literacy: Reading the Sacred in Everyday Life* (New York: Scribner, 1996), 367.

4. Brother David Steindl-Rast, *Gratefulness, The Heart of Prayer: An Approach to Life in Fullness* (Mahwah, NJ: Paulist, 1984), 12.

5. Wilkie Au, "The Practice of Gratitude" in *Presence: An International Journal of Spiritual Direction* (September 2011), 11.

6. Brian Doyle, *The Wet Engine: Exploring the Mad, Wild Miracle of the Heart* (Brewster, MA: Paraclete, 2005), 20–21.

7. Charles Clayman, ed, *The Human Body: An Illustrated Guide to Its Structure, Function, and Disorder* (New York: DK Publishers, 1995), 138.

8. Abraham Verghese, *Cutting for Stone* (New York: Vintage Publishing Company, 2010) 624.

9. Verghese, 624.

10. Gretchen White, *www.lifenut.com/blog/?p=1201*, May 23, 2008. Used by permission.

11. National Institute of Health, *kidney.niddk.nih.gov/kudiseases/pubs/yourkidney*, December 8, 2011.

12. Garabed Eknoyan, "The Kidneys in the Bible: What Happened?" in *Journal of the American Society of Nephrology* 16:12 (December 2005).

13. Philip Larkin, "Skin," *www.poetryconnection.net/poets/Philip_Larkin/4802*.

14. National Science Biomedical Research Institute, *nsbri.org/humanphysspace/focus6/ep_function.html*, December 22, 2011.

15. *Science Daily, www.sciencedaily.com/releases/2005/07/050718214954.htm*, December 23, 2011.

16. "Red Gold," Public Broadcasting System, *www.pbs.org/wnet/redgold/*, December 26, 2011.

17. Brother David Steindl-Rast, "Gratefulness: The Heart of Spiritual Direction," address given at annual conference of Spiritual Directors International, San Francisco, April 11, 2010.

18. Archbishop Desmond Tutu in *The Wisdom of Desmond Tutu*, ed. Michael Battle (Louisville, KY: Westminster John Knox Press, 2000), 36.

19. Water Science for Schools, United States Geological Survey, *ga.water. usgs.gov/edu/propertyyou.html*, December 28, 2011.

20. Wendell Berry, "The Pleasures of Eating" in Alice Peck, ed., *Bread, Body, Spirit: Finding the Sacred in Food* (Woodstock, VT: SkyLight Paths, 2008), 95.

21. Hunger in America, *www.worldhunger.org/articles/Learn/us_hunger_facts. htm*, December 29, 2011.

22. Peck, *Bread, Body, Spirit*, 89.

23. United States Department of Health and Human Services, *organdonor. gov/*, December 30, 2011.

24. Episcopal Church Archives, *www.episcopalarchives.org/cgi-bin/acts/acts_ resolution-complete.pl?resolution=1991-A097*, December. 31, 2011.